Product of a Misspent Youth

One Woman's Journey through Addiction, Mental Illness and Finding Beauty in Recovery

Melissa Palmer

ISBN 978-93-5883-037-8
© Melissa Palmer 2023

Published in India 2023 by Pencil

A brand of
One Point Six Technologies Pvt. Ltd.
Unit no. 26, Ground Floor, Building A1,
Wadala Truck Terminal Road,
Near Post Office, Antop Hill, Mumbai - 400037
E connect@thepencilapp.com
W www.thepencilapp.com

DISCLAIMER: *The opinions expressed in this book are those of the authors and do not purport to reflect the views of the Publisher.*

Author biography

Melissa is a wife, mother, stepmother, addict in recovery for the past 11 years, homeschool mom, secretary, a student with career diplomas in Wildlife and Forestry Conservation, Child Psychology, and Social Services Assistant with a Concentration in Substance Abuse, author, and owner of Moving Mountains Recovery Hotline. Melissa lives in the mountains of Western North Carolina. Melissa enjoys reading books, listening, and listening to documentaries. Melissa is the author of two books, Product of a Misspent Youth and Rise Above: A Guide To Recovery and Finding Strength in The Struggle. Melissa hopes to expand her hotline business into a store that sells shirts and merchandise with a recovery-based theme as well as an office where conversations can occur regarding recovery. Melissa is headstrong in guiding people through the recovery journey using her own experiences and what educational tools she has acquired over the years.

CONTENTS

Acknowledgements

It's no accident that I have lived long enough to write this book. This book not only represents me and what I have done, but it also represents what true love can do for a person. I want to thank my parents for never giving up on me and supporting me along the way, being such a huge part of my daughter's life, and just being there to pick up the pieces when I need you to. To my sisters, thank you for being there for me when I needed it. I want to thank every one of the guys mentioned in this book; if not for you, I would not be who I am today. I want to thank my mother-in-law for everything she has done for me thus far. I want my children to know that the mom you know now would not exist without you guys. You guys brought me back to life. I want to thank the few friends I managed to keep along this journey, and I want to show gratitude to the mother of my step-children; through a series of unfortunate circumstances, I got to know and love your children, and I am thankful that they did and that you guys are all a part of my story. Last but not least, that man that holds the key to my heart is my husband. If it hadn't been for your undying love, your wisdom, your patience, your unconditional love, I am confident that I do not think I would be in this world today. I also thank anyone that has assisted in publishing this book. I love you, everyone.

Thank you for believing in me, and don't ever give up on me because I'm not done yet.

Introduction

I want to thank whoever is about to read this book. The pages of this book contain bits and pieces of what is left of my heart and soul. Names have been changed to protect anonymity. I want to warn the reader that this book contains sensitive topics such as sexual abuse, domestic violence, and the use of drugs and alcohol. This is my story, some of the timing may be off, but everything I can remember is correct. Addiction and mental illness cause memory lapses and loss. This book is personal to me, and I open up in a way that, until now, I didn't think was possible. I hope you enjoy reading Product of a Misspent Youth.

CHAPTER 1

Hi, my name is Melissa, I am an addict in recovery, and this is my story. I was born in a small town in North Carolina in the summer of 1986. I was born to two loving parents who were both hard workers and always ensured I didn't go without. I was born an only child to them. My father had two more daughters from a previous marriage, Ann and Dawn. I saw both of them very often when I got older. We lived in that small town until I was two. When I was two, we moved out to Sassafras Mountain. My childhood, for the most part, was a happy one; growing up on Sassafras Mountain, which is the highest point of elevation in South Carolina, was a lot of fun. I can still smell the air from there; I would have to walk to and from the bus daily and take it all in. Where my home was located, put us right on the state line. It was a quiet, peaceful place unless our neighbors played live music or argued.I found solitude in walking around the woods of my neighborhood, taking in all the smells of the woods around me.I made friends with a couple of neighborhood dogs, and I had a beautiful dog by my side, he was part wolf and part chow, and I loved him. He, too, held a few childhood secrets of mine. I mainly spent my time learning all I could about my neighborhood. I'm sure I got on my neighbor's nerves often, but I enjoyed spending time with the older people. I would sit and listen to their stories, and they taught me how to play games like Scrabble; they were my friends back then, and they treated me like the child star of Sassafras; I would see them and show them the latest song or dance that I learned, and there was one time one of my neighbors let me sing and dance at a party they were having. It was so much fun, and so what if it was to the Spice Girls, they were hot then. The older people became like grandparents to me. A couple lived at the end of the road, and they were my oma and opa, my German grandparents; I loved them and enjoyed it when their grandkids would stay with them in the summer. That was the only time I was around other children outside of school, only twice were there any children in my neighborhood my age, and both times, they had to move after only a short time. Once again, I would be left alone to just my imagination. I grew up a very sheltered child and played with block people I had created from scrap wood that my dad would leave lying around the yard. My best friend was this little ole rag doll that someone got me when I was born, I named her Suzie, and to this day, she holds all my childhood secrets. When I started school, I began to make a few friends. One of my saddest memories was being taken out of class twice to say goodbye to a couple of girls moving out of state who had lived in my neighborhood. Every time I would get angry because I knew that, once again, I was all alone. I turned the bus driver into a diary and this big tall high schooler, a neighbor, into a close friend, Ben; we would talk the whole ride unless he were tired, then it was nap time. We were like that until he graduated. Then I was alone again. Once a group of brothers lived out there, but I wasn't close to them. It was just me and Ole Suzie. As I got older, I started to resent living out there because I felt I was missing out on so much. My parents went to work when I was old enough to leave alone. My dad always worked in construction for most of my life and worked in the hayfields, maintained our cattle, and grew a garden. my mom waited until I was old enough to go back to school to go back to work. I didn't mind it much, being home alone until summer, and I was out of school. I spent those days mainly watching tv and staying indoors, sometimes which would get me in trouble; though, a few years into me being left to my vices, my parents got satellite, and I was in heaven; I learned how to hook the phone cord into the back so I could rent pay per view movies and events, I got in trouble when they found out that I had rented Bride of Chucky and Woodstock '99. I was told then I was too smart for my good. I also called a psychic once; she told me I would die falling downstairs, and to this day, I am extra careful around them. That was a huge phone bill, and I believe my dad took the phone to work for a while. I just wanted someone to talk to, that's all. I was tired of talking with all my imaginary friends; looking back, I have to wonder if I was talking to my multiple personalities.I did manage to make one good friend, though, Sam, at least at the time I thought she was anyway. We met in 6th grade; she had just moved into my neighborhood. We hung out after school, and I would go to church with her and her mom on Wednesday nights. One day, we decided that I would get off the bus with her instead of getting off at my bus stop. We planned to hang out at her house for a while, but we decided to walk this trail beside her house and go to this abandoned shack nearby. When we got there we just sat down and hung out; we were smoking cigarettes then, I started stealing them from my dad. We hung out for over an hour until we heard my mother's voice calling for me; the school had called her and told her that I didn't get off the bus where I was supposed to have. I heard her and started to panic; Sam said we should probably head back to her house, so we did; as we were leaving, I tossed my cigarette out; being inexperienced, I just threw it down. We got not even a mile up the trail before we saw flames. I freaked out and started running back to her place. It wasn't long till we heard the fire trucks. The only trouble I got into was at school, and I wasn't allowed to hang out with her anymore. I didn't admit till years later that I was involved. As I got older, I was allowed to go and spend more time with my half-sisters. Ann would pick me up and take me to the carnival that came to town every year back then. That was when I was told about her lifestyle; I was 11 then and didn't understand what I had been told. I was very sheltered as a child. I can remember getting angry because I didn't understand. I figured it all out, though, and learned to accept it. I loved her and wanted her to be in my life. I was so lonely then that I would have accepted pretty much anything to have her stay in my life. As I said before, I didn't exactly grow up with either of my half-sisters, I did try to stay with them, and I did everything I could not to have to stay on that mountain all the time. My mom worked at a local summer camp for five years, and I learned so much and made friends with the other girls there. There was always something fun to do and something new to learn. I learned pottery and how to make jewelry, and I learned how to swim and kayak, and canoe; I even got to go whitewater rafting and rock climbing. I learned silly camp songs, gymnastics, and archery, which I discovered I was good at. There, at camp, I would discover that I had a love for two things, writing and reading books. Through writing, I found a release of everything, especially as I got older. Books, ah books, became my escape from everything. I would read any and everything I could get my hands on. Even though I could see my mom every day, I would get homesick. I guess she would tell the family because I received a letter from my uncle and one from my grandmother, that made me happy. I felt like all the other girls there, and it was great. They all seemed to have more exciting lives than I could; a couple were from across the waters. We even went and met with the guys for a coed end-of-summer dance. Camp was a great experience until a few days before summer camp was over, the last year I went, I would experience my first confusing sexual experience; I was awakened by something touching me in ways I had only seen in movies that I shouldn't have been watching, it was the girl Gina that slept in the bunk above mine, I knew it was her before I ever opened my eyes because she always smelled like french toast and syrup. I was frightened but stayed silent because I didn't want the director to find out and my mom would lose her job. To this day, the smell of French toast and syrup makes me sick. That was the last year I went to camp; I had gone for five years for the last two weeks of the summer. A couple weeks after camp ended, I started middle school. I liked school because I was away from home for the day but didn't exactly fit in with my peers. I wasn't athletic or super smart or even pretty, for that matter, not compared to the other girls. I fell into the outcast crowd. Mostly I was with a few select girls or selected guys; I liked the guys because they didn't judge you as much. They didn't care about your clothes or if you had makeup on. They were simple, and I could relate to them. The girls were all chatty and liked drama. Despite how my life has gone, I wouldn't say I like drama. I started to pull away from my parents more too. I managed through middle school with only a few minor crises, such as the car wreck with my parents. That year's end of middle school, I went to my first concert, Kiss, Ted Nugent, and Skid Row. That is a night that I won't forget. The summer before I was set to start my first year of high school, things would happen that would change me forever. That summer, I was allowed to travel with my oldest half-sister Dawn and her family to the coast of North Carolina. We were gone a whole week, a big deal to me since I had never really been out of my hometown at this time. I had a blast the entire time I was there. I was in awe of all the big dunes and the ocean. That's when I fell in love with the beach, and to this day, the beach is where I try to go to make sense of the chaos that my life sometimes seems to attract. As I said, I enjoyed the visit there, but the ride back quickly turned into a hellish experience. I was asleep in our van, the little kids with us and me.I took the back seat so I could have it all to myself. The little ones were behind my half-sister. There was a seat between the little ones and me, and it was taken by this 30-something-year-old man, Guy, that had tagged along on the trip. I was sleeping well when suddenly, a touch awakened me; the touch became more intense, and let me say that I was on my monthly at the time; I had started just before we left to head back home. I was just 13 years old. The experience lasted for far too long. I felt that I had to keep quiet. This was a grown man and a friend to my half-sister and her family. There were kids asleep, so I had to keep quiet. When it was over, I felt like my whole world had been shattered. I knew I could not tell anyone because, at that time, the one who had been abused was always blamed, so I stayed quiet. That year, I had acquired a boyfriend, Jarod, my first real boyfriend. I had one the previous year, my first kiss, but he became a close friend instead. The guy I had started dating was unlike the other guys in our school, he seemed more mature and a couple of years older than me, but he was more mature than most of the guys I went to school with. We spent the summer talking on the phone and hung out a couple of times. The summer ended, and I started high school in 2000. I started first year very differently than I had in years past. then, I began having severe headaches and had to go to the emergency department to receive treatment, my introduction to iv pain meds. I have suffered from migraines since. I spent several years getting pain shots because of them with no real results. My first year would be one of my worst years during my entire school days. Within the first month of school, I experienced the first real monumental loss, my great-grandmother. She was buried on my 14th birthday. It was also that day that one of the most horrific events to date would happen to me, on my birthday, in the back of my mother's car, I was raped for the first time. I was devastated and confused. I thought Jarod loved me, but that was far from the truth. It was a long time before I said anything to anyone about it. I tried to tell my few friends, but nobody believed me. After the rape, I began a very toxic, confusing relationship with him that lasted on and off for a couple of years. He ended up quitting school about midyear, and it was then that I would take some pills for the first time other than my mom's sleeping pills or doctor prescribed. Because they were from a store, I thought they might be safe, and when a couple of guys gave them to me, I took them. They were just yellow jackets, store speed essentially. I got them so that I could study for our final exams, but instead of feeling all jacked up, I walked into my classroom, was immediately sick, and was taken to the hospital to have my stomach pumped. That was the first time I overdosed. Going back to school after that was pure hell; if I wasn't getting picked on for that, I was getting picked on by the friends of the person who had raped me. My life was a living hell at this point; I was so confused and upset about everything that I would cause myself to develop eating disorders. I was either one extreme or the next. I can remember when my aunts figured out that I was bulimic and had a stern talk with me. My moods and behavior were the same way; I was unpredictable back then. I convinced Jarod to steal his dad's truck, and we ran to the nearest state. In my mind, we were going to get married, but once my parents saw I was gone, they drove to SC to bring me back home. We were arrested and placed into a holding cell. I was so delusional back then, and he convinced me that it wasn't rape, and that I didn't mean to say no, I was just confused. I turned on my parents then, I even ripped the necklace I bought Mama for her birthday off her neck; the necklace read #1; Mom and I told her she didn't deserve that title as I ripped it off her neck. That is when I demanded they let me move out, and I did, I moved in with him, the one who clouded every responsible thought I should have had. I stayed there for a week until the school called my parents about my absence.

I went back home after that. I can remember being so depressed, so confused. this was when I began to cut myself; I needed a release, an escape. I would attend an alternative school in the second half of my first year. My habit of skipping school didn't improve, but I was happier there. I had been suspended from my previous school and had to do community service and go counseling for taking drugs on school property. Counseling, I found to be a lot of fun. there was no way I could be frank with them, so I told them what they wanted to hear. I say that because by that time I started to see them, I learned that I had a way with words, and I was smart enough that I could write down everything I had experienced as far as my symptoms go and match it with a diagnosis and the meds i needed to help with it. Which is all I would go by. I knew I was depressed; I knew that I wanted to end my life just about every other day and that it wasn't just normal teenage stuff; this was real; I knew that my moods change like the wind; I knew that all I wanted to do is sleep and hope that I didn't wake up. By the time I saw my first psychiatrist, I had been stealing my mother's prescription sleeping pills, anything to knock me out, and the nightmares and flashbacks I was experiencing. I knew how to "con" the Doctors into giving me whatever I wanted, but I didn't consider the side effects of each medication I was getting. In time, I was put on several medications, each one having a different effect. I was either a teen zombie and couldn't keep my eyes open long enough to do anything, or I was completely jacked up and so weird that I was almost uncontrollable. During all this, I would temporarily lose my sister, Ann, she had been living a hectic life for several years, and it would catch up with her; I still remember the day she went to jail, and it was a long time before I saw her again. Communication wasn't that great between us either, I felt like she had abandoned me for her friends, and it would be years before we would work through everything. Most of my sophomore year was spent in a haze. I skipped school a lot because I didn't feel I could function in class, so I just wouldn't go. I would make my time up on Saturdays instead, go before school, or stay after when I went. I didn't make horrible grades in school, though I know I could have done better. That year I would play with mushrooms one morning before school forcing me to get up and walk out after the waterfalls were falling all around me (my English class had a waterfall mural). I left school and would go hang out with this guy who had quite a bad reputation; that experience would lead me to meet my best friend; she just happened to be at the restaurant across from the high school when my parents came looking for me. At this point, we didn't know each other that well, so she felt she didn't need to cover for me about my not being in school. Our parents bowled in the same league, so we knew who each other was but not much else. I WAS FURIOUS when I found out she was the one who ratted me out. I wanted to fight her, but I didn't; instead, we talked, and from that moment on, for the last 22 years, she held the position of best friend and non-biological sister. My least pleasant memory from that point in my life is the night of dance at school. It was sweetheart, and though I had gotten all dolled up and went, I made the huge mistake of leaving. I had a couple of friends take me to a house where Jarod, the guy who raped me on my birthday, was living, the guy who I had run away with. The one who, for what seemed like a lifetime, I was obsessed over in such a toxic way. I know, "Why be around him if he raped you?" well, the truth is he convinced me that it wasn't rape; in my 15-year-old brain, I believed it, I believed that I wanted that experience to happen, though when it did, I was still a virgin, technically, yes I had been messed with before but not in that way. I trusted him, even though I loved him, but that night, everything would change. I got to his place, and many people were there; they were drinking, partying wide open. I had not drunk anything stronger than wine before, but I got too drunk that night to realize what was happening to me. He told me I could go and lie down in his room, and I did. I was ready to pass out when he got on top of me and began. I tried to scream no and must have, even though nobody came in to rescue me; they only turned the music up. Today, I will turn the radio off or leave the store. If that song comes on, I can't handle it. After that experience, I became completely withdrawn. I wish I could say that the rape was the worst part of the situation, but that is far from the truth, about 2.5 months afterward, I found out I was pregnant. 15 and pregnant was not something I saw for myself, but I decided to do my best to handle the situation. I told Jared, who told his uncle, who in turn told me I was not going to ruin their family and took me to Asheville, lied to them and told them he was my legal guardian and signed for me to have an abortion. I was relieved and emotionally destroyed at the same time. After that, I was never the same. At that point in my life, I didn't care what happened to me. All the issues I had before with eating disorders returned with a vengeance.That night and the next morning stayed on repeat in my head, and I could still see everything; I was still wearing the dress when I was brought back to my grandparent's house. I couldn't even look at them; I was filled with that much shame. The school had become hell on earth by then; some guys there had told people what happened, it wasn't the truth, of course, but it was out there. I tried to tell the truth, and nobody took me seriously, so I started to shut down. I talked only with my counselor about what had happened, and that was very little; I mainly sat in there and cried. I wrote about it, but mostly, I cut myself. My arms still hold the scars where I cut them. The scars are a constant reminder of all the pain I endured growing up and how I will do everything I cannot to return to that place. Junior year was spent in a mixture of drugs, alcohol, and skipping school. I can remember getting into a fight with a couple of girls; the first fight I ever got into was with this girl who I always thought of as a hateful bully, we got into a fight because I slept with her boyfriend, who, in my defense, told me they were broken up, I took the hit like a champ, and we became friends afterward. The second was because I told a girl's parents she was on meth. Again I took the hit. I felt like I did the right thing and told her I hoped hitting me made her feel better. I spent most of my time hanging with various people, we would gather at the restaurant across the street and either go to the park or another friend's house. That was also when I would meet this GA boy who took my defiance to a whole new level, I would end up having my first real dealings with the law and have an officer talk to me and plant the idea in my head that I could make it out and become someone, but I didn't believe him because I was already so damaged. I never wanted to be at my parents' place. I wouldn't say I liked it there. He had been there, and everything reminded me of him. I would stay with friends or, if I got lucky, with my half-sister Ann, who had recently returned to my life. I enjoyed those weekends because she was so carefree. As long as I did not get too out of hand, I was allowed to let loose and have fun. I also had fun with her roommates; we would drink and dance around in her living room. That was the only time I was happy. I don't know how I managed to make it through, but I did and started my senior year of high school in the fall of 2003. The first half of senior year began with my having all of my wisdom teeth taken out and my intro to prescription pain pills. I took them until the prescription was gone, then started figuring out how to get my hands on more.I didn't take my senior year seriously, I enjoyed my English class and the video learning class I was taking, but other than that, I wouldn't say I liked school. I was still doing any drug I could get and drinking whatever I could. I was wild and didn't care as long as I could feel numb.That September, my best friend would have her first child, and a series of events would bring us close together and tear us apart. In December of 2003, I met and instantly fell for this gorgeous blond-haired guy, Brendon; I met him in the hallway of the local mall, we locked eyes, and that's all she wrote; we began a whirlwind romance that would ultimately end in devastating heartbreak. He knew I had a problem with drugs, and during my senior year, he would show up and whisk me away from all my friends in the hopes that I would get clean. His efforts did have their reward; I began to care more about my grades, started hanging out with a different group of friends, and even entered my first poetry contest and received an honorable mention; I went with the rest of my senior class on our senior trip. I had a blast, I experienced New York City for the first time and fell in love, and that spring, we had a very memorable night; he had never gone to his medical. It at my senior pr had quit school, so I wanted the night to be spe though I'm sure he had much rather been at the Metallica concert instead. For the most part, Senior year would be my best year of school yet, despite having to go out the last week of school to have my appendix removed. During that week of recovery, I took more pain pills to push through and walk without hurting myself. The night before graduation, I was surprised with kid rock concert tickets. I had a blast despite tearing my stitches a little bit. The next morning though, I was proud to walk across the stage and graduate from high school in 2004. I originally planned to move and go to community college in Whittier, where I spent most of my time. I had been spending time with his family, who had agreed to let me stay with them and go to community college. Things were pretty serious between him and me. We even got engaged. I still have the wedding dress that I bought. After graduating that day, I planned to move to Asheville instead and live with my half-sister. I was furious, but that was the cards dealt to me, so I moved in with her the same day after we celebrated my graduation and started a whole new chapter in my life. I was officially headed to the big city of Asheville, Nc. I would have the whole world at my fingertips, or so I thought.

CHAPTER 2

It is the summer of 2004, and I am 17 years old. I am living with Ann in Asheville, Nc. I have only visited a big city at this point, and getting around by foot or bus was a constant challenge. I'm constantly getting lost when I try to go anywhere alone, but I got a job at Mcdonalds, my first job. Asheville was great, but getting used to nothing but buildings and roads was hard. This is about when I would disappear for a few days; well, to begin with, I never intended to return, but I would take my graduation money and buy a bus ticket to none other than New York City. I hung out at Grand Central Station trying to figure out a plan; back then, I wasn't as responsible as I am now, so essentially, I didn't have an actual plan. I hoped it would go like an episode of "Friends" and I would take up with some great people and never look back to NC. I spent close to a week there before deciding that I wouldn't run into "Rachel, Ross, or Joey" and I doubted that it wouldn't be that easy to make friends there, especially since everyone just looked so mean. God forbid speaking to anyone, so I got a ticket home.Everyone around me was oblivious to my newfound release, but the truth is that I was hiding a little secret; I had a stash of pills left over from my appendix surgery and went from taking them orally to snorting them up my nose. I was instantly hooked to the immediate high that I got from it, and quickly, it became a habit for me, a bad one. I made friends with some guys at work and got them almost daily. Nobody really knew what I was doing, or at least that's what I was telling myself, but the people around me knew and tried to help me, but I just pushed them away. One day, while I was off work, I started to make friends with a guy that had been staying at Ann's house with her roommate; he had this pipe and clear stuff in it; I had never seen anything like it at that time so naturally, my curiosity rose, and at 17 years old, I discovered Meth. hooked immediately, I began using meth every chance I got, along with the pills I was still calling and by the end of that summer, I was addicted. I noticed it was taking over my thoughts and actions; I started doing things I had told myself I would never do. One day, I left work with the guys I had been getting my drugs from, and we started walking. I thought they were going to walk me home, back to Anns, but we were going in the wrong direction for that. I was so out of it by the time I realized, but I didn't care; I didn't care until Ann's car pulled up to us. I began cursing her out because, well, I don't know. I guess it didn't occur to me that she was saving my life; I later found out they were taking me to a "trap house," but I was cussing her out, and finally, I got in the car, she took me straight to my mom and dads, back out to the mountain, and for a while, the city life was over for me. While at my parents, I got a job working where my mom worked. I would still go to Asheville on my days off and Brendon, but he quickly caught on to my drug habits and started to distance himself from me. It broke my heart, and I would drown the pain with more drugs, either prescribed or not. Right before my 18th birthday, I began to experience a lot of pain and sickness; I hadn't told anyone I had been on meth, so everyone thought it was just pills. Still, I was admitted to the hospital and hooked up to a morphine pump, which was like heaven to me, a constant high and constant numbness, which I craved by this point. Nonetheless, I kept calling Brendon; he had enough of me and my issues by then. I couldn't help it; I turned into this psycho ex. We finally broke up while I was in the hospital, but only because my family couldn't stand to watch me go through the pain and torture that I kept putting myself through; they thought it was all him; the truth is, I'm the only one who had that shovel. Ever since I was 14, if someone gets close to me, I push them away. I don't want to be hurt again. At 18, I had a broken heart, and it was time to move on with my life. After I recovered from my hospital stay, I started living with my parents full time, which meant being there all the time, seeing "him" everywhere, smelling "him." the first rule of life, is don't bring boyfriends home and have sleepovers. I had that bad habit, hell I was lonely out there, of course, I would have them spend the night; my parents had a rule, though, unless I was married, none of them were allowed to sleep in my room; it was couch or dads office where he could keep a close eye on things. All the memories, though, I took it as long as I could, then started to try and go out and about. My dad was in the local bowling league, so I would go with him to have fun and see who I could mingle with. It wasn't long after I started going that I met another guy who was much older than me, Kent. We started to hang out and talk, and one thing led to another, and before I knew it, I was living there most of the time. That fall, my best friend would have her son, I was so happy, but I couldn't enjoy it because I had gotten myself into a situation Kent was a bit controlling but sweet.He moved fast, though; he showed up at my oldest sister's house one day that I was there and asked me to marry him. I didn't know what to say, so I replied with I don't know, I may have said yes, but I changed my mind after I had time to think. He noticed I had a drug problem and worked with my parents to get me help. By this time, drugs weren't my only problem, I had learned that I was suffering from depression, anxiety, and PTSD, but none of those explained the extreme highs or extreme lows I was experiencing. I could go from smiling to being ready to fight or cry in the blink of an eye. It didn't matter what it was about; it was just that quick. So I went to a mental hospital for the first time, not knowing what I was up against. The experience was horrific. During this stay, I was diagnosed as having bipolar disorder and borderline personality disorder. I don't know how long I was there, but when I got out, it seemed like my life was being planned out for me. I had a place to live, not my parents house; my mom had to sit me up with everything I would need to be on my own. I wasn't alone, though, I was living with Kent, and things went well for a while until they didn't. He started to control who I talked to and where I went, even slept in front of the door to keep me inside; he started to abuse me more than just physically and even told me he was going to kill me and take me to where he was from which conveniently happens to be my last name at the time and the state he came from. I immediately knew that things had become dangerous for me. I devised a plan that I believed would be foolproof to save me, and it was to some degree. The morning I was "taking my last ride," I convinced him to let me go to my parent's house and grab some things; what I grabbed saved my life. I took as much of my mom's jewelry and gave it to him to pawn for "gas money." Yes, I made him think I was a willing participant in my demise, but I gave it to him and told him to go into the pawn shop and pawn it, claiming I lost my ID. Once he was in the pawn shop, I made a phone call to my Ann, who called my mom and set everything into motion. I told him I wanted to hook back up with Brendon and smooth-talked my way into him, letting him out of the vehicle. He left me at a restaurant on the side of the interstate, but not before he held a knife to my throat and told me that he would finish the job one day. I trembled as I heard those words but safely got away and ran into the restaurant where I called my Ann, who called my mom, who called his probation officer, which resulted in him being arrested and sent to prison. I can thank those gals for that day; thinking quickly saved my life. I was out of the woodwork in the legal aspect, though I was set to face charges for felony robbery at 18 years old. My day in court finally arrived, and I was offered a plea deal where I would plead guilty to the lesser charge of misdemeanor theft; I took it and received probation and community service. I didn't mind the probation, except that I would have to return to my parent's house on the mountain. Like many times before, being out there worked for a while, but I got away again to stay with some friends to complete my community service. I finished that in the spring of 2005 and moved back in with my parents. This stay, too, would be short-lived. I will meet the next chapter in my story one night at the bowling alley. The chapter that I like to refer to as my 1st mistake

CHAPTER 3

It is the spring of 2005. I am 19, on probation, and living with my parents on the mountain. As I said, I hated being stuck on the mountain day in and day out, so I would jump at the chance to escape every chance I took. My best friend would come to rescue me, and me her and the kids would go for rides and hang out; those are some of my favorite moments, especially the night at wendys when we all got into a food fight, the baby started it when he threw his fries, and we just continued, we cleaned up our mess of course and had fun. The other chance came once or twice a week when my dad would go to the bowling alley during league night. One night I went with him and, like all of the other times, headed straight for the game room. Normally I would just watch the guys play pool and listen to the jukebox or play video games there, but tonight, something, or rather someone caught my eye. He had dark hair and dark eyes and was so sweet. Jamie, he made me laugh, which was something I didn't do anymore. We exchanged numbers, and he called me every night. We started hanging out outside the bowling alley, like at his friends houses. I saw then that I could get whatever I wanted from him; he had the same habits I did. So began a whirlwind romance. My parents couldn't stand him, but he had a bad boy image, and I took it all in. A few things from the start should have been red flags, but if they were, I ignored them. All I knew was that I was on probation and wanted out of my parent's house. Sometime that June, I called and told him I had had enough and wanted him to get me. He did, and the rest is a blur. I just know that I woke up in a hotel in town and asked him what was going on, and that's when I was informed that I had gotten married for the first time. From day one, it was the survival of the fittest marriage. We were always hungry; there were several nights that we didn't have anywhere to sleep; other times, we would end up with some of his family, which was worse most of the time than not having anywhere to go. That first summer was a hard one; we lived in a tent for most of it in various places like the forest or people's yards. He never had a job for long; that was one thing he would have a car, but no job, a job but no car, or neither. There was no happy medium. There was no happiness at all, at least not real happiness. Things would be ok once he got paid until the money ran out and we ran out of pills. He would get so bad that he would either hurt himself or hurt me so we could get pain pills from the local drs and hospitals. There were many days we spent with the Doctor; I believe shopping is the right term, but we would have a few people, and someone would get hurt and go in to get a script. All the pain shots while in there was just a bonus, but we would come back with at least a script each. One time he got pulled over though, and was arrested, I stayed with the vehicle until someone got me, I was right off the interstate and terrified the whole time. When we all got scripts, whoever went one party time; for me, meant watching him get wasted and that trip supplies out. There were some nights that we would sit up and talk through the highness, it was usually the coming down point that we would start to argue about this or that. At one point in early fall, we stayed at my parents house. We were working on a car that he had bought. He figured out that he needed extra help so we went to some of his families to get the help he needed to fix it. The car was fixed in the early morning hours and he had the bright idea to take it for a test drive. I woke up to a huge tree with ems trying to get me out of my seatbelt. He had fallen asleep and we wrecked head-on straight into a tree head-on in somebody's front yard. I was black and blue all over. We were taken to the hospital, which was a big fight with everyone. I don't remember much from that night but I do know I was at the police station; I threw something at their doors and was arrested for disorderly conduct, from jail, I went back to the hospital. I had a concussion. The Doctors gave me constant pain pills because of my back and head. The rest of the summer became a nightmare. He would make me do things that I will never utter into words and he was violent back then too. Over time though things would take a turn for the worse; by the fall of that year, we were living in a house that we rented by the room, not the whole house, just a room. In the beginning things seemed ok, I would go with him to work and learn how to make furniture, and we were happy for the most part. We still depended on other people for rides and things, but we were making it for once. One night, he wanted pills badly; he had tried every way he could and got nowhere. He looked at me and said "Stab me, don't kill me, just cut me a little " I thought he seriously lost his mind. I did it, though; I got him good, too, next thing I know, he's holding the wound spot and running out the door. I'm not kidding when I say that he went to the end of the street then back, making sure he bled on the way. When he got back to the steps, I was told to call 911 and say that he had been robbed at knifepoint. I literally hid his wallet under our mattress. Anyway, it worked, though I don't think that the cops believed the story, he got what he was after and all was well again. Later that fall, I got a job at a nearby fast-food joint. My probation officer said I had to or get violated so I got a job, my second job ever. I did ok there except for when he would take all my tips for pills, and I couldn't eat, the only time I got to eat anything was at work. I was always broke. The one time I tried to protest, he grabbed me by the wrist so hard that it left a bruise. I didn't last there too long after we were kicked out of the house and went to stay with his family. There the abuse got worse, i wasn't allowed to eat anything, and every dime we made went to drugs. That Christmas was horrible, he made me return everything I got. It would be that way for two years, so he would have drug money, anything that he would buy, I would have to sell or pawn. Like a game system we bought to "bring us closer together." I remember it was cold and raining one December day and I was again going to stay somewhere I didn't know the person, just that they were his family. I hated living like this; I was still 19 this time and couldn't do it anymore. I had court in January of 2006 from some recent assault charges from Jamie, and I activated my sentence to spend 45 days in the county jail. When I made the decision to activate my sentence, I thought that I had thought everything through. I had a good reason to be here. I am 19 years old, homeless, hungry, and weigh 98 lbs. I was seriously dying inside; I needed that break from the outside. I needed to get away from him truthfully. What I wasn't prepared for was the sound of that door slamming shut or sharing a shower with other chicks or going to the bathroom in front of everyone. Or the loneliness that I would feel for the next 45 days. He would visit and write letters and the occasional phone call, but after 31 days, on February 18, 2006, (my moms birthday), I was released unexpectedly. I will never forget that moment when they popped the door and told me I was evicted. Would you believe I tried to argue with them! I complied, though, and when that door unlocked, my mom was waiting for me at the end of the hallway. I was so happy to see her; I hugged her neck and thought I was finally going home; boy, was I wrong? There was a surprise waiting for me down the road, Ann, which meant I went back to Asheville, I guess she thought she could save me. This time was different though; she had moved out of the city and to a small place on the outskirts. I got a job and even returned to school for the first time since high school. I had spent a night talking things out with a mall guy just to discover that I was attracted to girls. At least for the moment I was anyway. I had gone out with a variety of guys, and at that moment in my life Lynn was what I needed. I moved out of Ann and in with Lynn for a spell, we got kicked out of her place, and both got jobs that came with a housing option up on the Blue Ridge Parkway at a cute little place called Pisgah Inn. I finally felt home there, something that was foreign to me. I embraced everything the inn had to offer and did well until my luck turned sour when I had an incident at work and had to be rushed to the hospital. My gallbladder had ruptured so I went for emergency surgery to remove it. I didn't let a week pass until I went back to work. I enjoyed my job, the people, everything. I was home there. I had locked eyes with a red headed stranger Kraig, on my first day, and we had exchanged innocent flirts here and there, but on my first night back, Kraig brought me a slice of cake from somebody's birthday party and we talked till the late hours. After that, we were practically inseparable. I broke up with Lynn and moved straight in with Kraig. He was perfect, smart, charming, good looking. He was everything I needed then. As the season went on, I started drinking heavily. There were nights I would black out and have no clue what I had done or what had been because of that, I ended up getting a nasty spider bite. I had a microwave to cook in, that's it, it was so tiny you turn it twice, and you're both in and out of it. We fought constantly, and every other week, one of us was going to jail for beating the other one. I will not lie and say it was all his fault. That's what led me to leave the inn. I got drunk and couldn't explain my actions so I was let go. I still have no real memory of that night. Kraig was mad at me, so I knew whatever I had done must have been bad. I placed the call home, back to that mountain I used to feel was my prison. I moved back home the summer of 06 once again, and something would take me away. This time it was in the form of my then-husband, whom I had almost forgotten existed, Jamie. He called me one day out to my parents, and I just happened to answer. He wanted to talk, he said; I agreed and picked him up. I guess I'm a glutton for punishment by this point but I agree to go back. Immediately it was the same ole thing; this time, we had our place, this tin box rundown camper in a trailer park. When I say this place was the things nightmares are made of, I mean that there were huge holes in the bathroom, ulta, because it wasn't; I was just as at fault.

There were days he would come in just messed up out of his gourd, and I'd throw something at him just trying to piss him off. Little by little, I had been sending my things home with mom so that when I left I would only need a backpack. Deep down, I knew that it was time for me to leave, for good this time. That day finally came that fall. I had gone to my dr for some reason, and he told me that i was pregnant, i was 20 at this time. The thought of having my first child, I was happy but frightened at the same time. I planned a dinner to tell him when he started yelling at me, telling me he didn't believe me, i showed him the test, then he tried to say the baby didn't belong to him. I was heartbroken and furious; I packed my backpack and started to leave, that's when he hit me and I left. I must have taken out charges on him because we were in court when I started to feel pain like I never felt before. I was rushed to the hospital where they said that I might be having complications in my pregnancy due to the stress of everything. I was sent home after that and decided I wanted a divorce. I remember him telling me he had been married before so I checked into it and found out that he was still married in 05 when he married me. My ticket to freedom, I gave him the choice of signing or face charges for bigotry and he signed. After all, I didn't have enough evidence to show he was the cause of my losing my unborn son.I'll never forget that day, i took the stand and told my side of the story only to have his attorney tear up. He knew I was right about the abuse; I had those records, but linking the abuse as the sole cause of my unborn son's death, just wasn't impossible. I remember vividly, hitting the floor in hysteria because, at the time, that was the only emotion I could feel. I thought that once the marriage was over and going to court, that I would be ok for a while and that it would be the end of my troubles. I would soon find out that I would be sadly mistaken. Halloween night 06, I was trick-or-treating with Dawn and her family when I started to hurt really bad. I hadn't been feeling well for days, so I thought that I would go and get checked out to see if the baby was ok.This young, I didn't comprehend everything that was going on. I didn't understand that I lost him a month ago but found out the next day that not only had I lost him, I had been carrying his dead fetus for a month, setting up to convince myself that I would never be a mother to anyone. Sometimes, I would ask myself what's a dangerous infection. They performed a D-N-C on me to finish getting everything out of me. I was devastated. They had given me something for the pain and the emotional trauma, and I mixed alcohol and pills for the next two months.I would stay at Dawn's house, and I always had my bottle of Jack Daniels and a bottle of anxiety pills that the doctor gave me to "help me cope" after discharge. at that point, i was a Freebird; I stayed with whoever and did whatever I didn't care, was in pain, my heart was broken. There were times when I would make a living. I wanted to be with my son, so what if I hadn't held him, I didn't care, that baby was my true first love. I hate to think about what he would have grown up in, but he would have been my baby boy. Dawn held my hand when the doctors finally made me realize that I lost him; she cried with me and then helped me to move past it. I will forever be grateful for everything she has done for me. I was bouncing around a lot, eventually, I hooked back up with the Kraig, and even he could not handle me. I was wild and out to get mine no matter who I hurt.This would lead to a few things, the first being a great relationship with a guy named Phipps; he truly became a breath of fresh air to me. I met him at my oldest sister's house, and we clicked immediately. He didn't really say much about my drinking or drug usage; he just let me be me. I don't recall why we parted ways. I'm sure I pulled a houdini or something. My best friend told me that this was also when I would have to disappear for days and shrescue myself. I truly thank God for her every day. One night though, neither my best friend nor Phipps could save me, I would be a fucking dumb ass, pardon my French, but i was that night; I let myself get drunk and let my guard down, seriously one of the worst mistakes I have ever made, i was hanging out in this jeep with three guys, we were all pretty lit, and I began to kiss one of them, before I knew it, all three of them were around me, that night i was raped by all three of them. That night Melissa DIED; I have never been the same since. I didn't go back to my sisters for a long time after that, and telling her was not an option, not sure it will ever be an option. I would go back to my parent's house which was where I was for a weekend when I ran into my non-serious first boyfriend, i called him "my fro," and through school, we became good friends, one of the best guys friends I ever had, so I agreed to hang out with him and he talked me into going to this bar out of town and letting loose a little. That's where I would meet this fun-loving guy with whom I would spend the next 6 years, beginning a whole new chapter in my story.

CHAPTER 4

It is the winter of 2006; I am not yet 21, but hanging out at this bar then was a happening place. That night I went with a perfect guy friend from school, who I knew I would be safe around. Though I wasn't 21, I managed to get pretty drunk quickly. I had my first sex on the beach, and for a while, that was my drink of choice. I was having fun for the first time in a long time. I was dancing the night away when I noticed this guy had just slid behind me dancing. I went with it cause hell, that's what I was there for, to have fun. The song ended and he introduced himself, "Hi, my name is Kenton" I laughed, and the night went on. He may have bought me a drink or two, I couldn't honestly say now, but there was some connection between us, despite our age difference. The night ended and I went back to the mountain. I learned my new goal would be not to drink and ride that night. That next week I saw Kenton again at the bowling alley. He was in the same bowling league my dad was in. We started to hang out more and more. I even went to his place to hang out. He seemed very gentle, kind, funny, and had a sense of grit. Always smiling, always positive, I thought ok, maybe this will work after all. I knew he liked to have the same kind of fun that I did, but he was kept on the down low and not often. I moved in with him after a month or so of hanging out. Yes, I moved fast, but I was always running from those memories, the smells of that place, and everything that happened there. I often moved in with the guy after a short time of knowing him, I was lonely and wanted out of that house on the mountain. I moved in with him, and things were going great for a while. He took me to get all my stuff from the red-headed stranger and I began a new life. We had fun; I went to work with him, talked, and laughed; I was thrilled. He even took me to the beach once; I drank the whole time and can't remember much of it. I do know that, for once; I felt love. I felt safe in his arms, even if they held me in the ocean. I spent that Christmas with his family, with the night ending with us listening for Santa at the jail, I thought it was quite cool, I got to hang out there and not be an inmate. I knew they had heard about me, and I tried to go through one of them when I was married to the first mistake, they surprised me at my parents house, thought they were going to take me to a hospital, for some reason, my mom had called them, I ended up going to the mental part of the ed and talking my way right back out. I left with my best friend and learned just how much hatred she had for the current ass I was married to. The holidays would come and go, and in February of 2007, I would experience a tragic loss, and instead of being there for someone I loved deeply, I chose to get high. It was February 7, 2007, and I was up early; at the time, Kenton and I were living with his brother, who just so happened to be a police officer; he came in close to 8 o'clock that morning and had just had a look about him, I asked what was wrong, and he told me that a toddler had been killed by his step-father the night/ early morning hours of the night before, I was said "that's horrible," I said "Melissa, go to your best friend, it was her son," I lost it, I think I called mama to come get me, but I went straight to her side. She was still in shock, but I was able to put the pieces together. The days that follow are a blur; I took a turn down a road straight toward hell. Kenton was teaching me how to drive at the time, and things were ok until the day I took his truck; while he was out of town, I called him and told him I was going to the gas station just right up the road. I was going to meet Jamie to get some pills from him. I never made it, instead, I wrecked on a back road, taking out a state sign and going into a ditch, hitting a tree, and totaling Kenton's truck. Boy, was I in trouble, but not as much trouble as I was about to be in, I would have one hell of a screw-up. This next tidbit is one big blur, I will state only what I remember to be accurate for this book. To start with, after I totaled the truck, I wanted to get away from everyone. I was grieving in ways I could not explain and needed out. I made a phone call to Jamie, told him what was going on and I wanted him to pick me up. I knew he was always good for something extra too. So yes, that was my connection to him, but I swear to God my intentions were just to talk and score that high I wanted. I got that high plus more than I had bargained for, though, I really should have known better. I guess it was a Friday when I left because I woke up that morning on Sunday and looked around at my surroundings. I was in a hotel; I was like, oh no, not again, no hell no. I picked up the phone and did what most girls do. I called Mama. I asked her what was going on because somehow mama always knew what I was doing, even when i didn't, but this time she said, "You tell me" I, of course, had no explanation other than I need to get away. I told her that all I wanted to do was talk about the first mistake.

It was at that time that the first mistake rose and said, "What you mean what is going on here" I said, "where am I, and what am I doing here with you" his reply with a shit-eating grin was "well darling you're in Tennessee, and you've married again," I responded with " bullshit, not today satan, not today, the hell we are, i want to go home right now" my mother is in my ear the entire time telling me to "hurry up and get your ass back here." I was trying to process everything, and apparently, we stopped and got this medicine used for anxiety. It is the same med I was taking the first time I married his ass.I call it the blackout pill and refuse to take it now. I told him then, "Take me home now; I'll die before I stay married to you". He smiled that evil smile and agreed to take me back to North Carolina, though I thought he was going to kill me on the ride back; I made it back safe, though and got the marriage annulled quickly. It's what I call (viva las Sevierville). I closed that chapter and never looked back to him. I began to pick up the pieces from that whole nightmare which would be when I agreed to go to rehab for the first time. I was there three days when I called home and a family member told me that my grandfather was dying in the hospital. I left that night and went straight to his side. I was there just a few minutes before he took his last breath. I immediately ran out of the hospital straight to my mother's car and stole what meds I could numb me. I was close to my grandfather; he was one of my favorite people to be around. I learned a lot from him and enjoyed hearing stories about the war and his childhood and who in the family belongs to whom. I was just fascinated by him, so it destroyed a piece of my heart when he passed. I used him as an excuse to drink and stay messed up all the time for a long time. It was a combination of losses and everything I had already been through. Nonetheless, I was partying almost 7 days a week. I stayed in that drunken haze for several years, I guess. It started when I moved in with Kenton full time and continued through two more moves, each time our house being the party house, he became my enabler. We had a blast, though; I was experiencing things I had never really experienced, and all in the name of fun. I did do some productive things during this time, or at least I attempted to anyway. I got a couple of different jobs; I never made any money though; I had to pay Kenton for the truck I totaled. For the most part, life wasn't too bad; I fell into a routine of work, school, friends, partying. that is until I made a horrible mistake one day and accepted a ride from work from Jarod, the guy who raped me when I was a teenager. I know, I've got to be dumb right, the answer is yes, I was dumb and naive, and I believed his apology and started to trust him. Bad mistake, instead of taking where I said I needed to go, he said I needed to ride with him to dump the load of trees he had on his truck. I thought nothing really about it and we kept talking. I would learn he was married with a child on the way. I was genuinely happy for him even after all we went through. We got to the dump site, and he put the truck in park and raped me agian; this time, I tried harder to fight back since i was sober that day and had the strength to. He finished then went to do what he was there to do. I couldn't believe I had been this stupid, this naive to trust him again. He dropped me off and this time I went to the police; I went to the hospital and did the rape kit, but they still didn't believe my story, and in time the detective gave back my clothes from that day and said that they didnt do the rape kit and are taking his word. I was destroyed at that time, i had been raped three times by the same person, and no body believed me. After that I left where I was working and went to work at a restaurant down the road. I liked that job other than when he would come in, or his friends harassed me. There were a few nights that I would have to find a ride to the alley where the fun guy was and it wasn't a problem. This one night, I had gotten off early so I was going to walk to the alley where everyone else was. I decided to have a drink first. I didn't think about protecting my drink or anything back then, i ordered it and went to the bathroom; when I came back, my drink was on the bar waiting on me, I finished it and stood up, i was woozy, but I remember thinking that the bartender must have made the drink extra strong, i began the walk to the alley, but before I could get out of the parking lot, i was picked up by a dark man with an accent, he took me to his truck, one of those Mayflower delivery trucks and he raped me, I was in and out of it for most of the ordeal but I remember waking up once to see a phone, he was filming it. I couldn't fight back, I couldn't do anything. When he was done, he threw me out of the truck and shut the door. I have no memory of the rest of that night. Kenton what happened and of course he didn't believe me, I told no one after that. I continued to work at the restaurant until I was fired one day for not showing up to work when scheduled. Hell, I didn't care if I worked or not. I was taking a math class at a local community college and I dropped out. Nothing mattered to me anymore. I didn't want to live much less anything else. The only person in my life I trusted was Mack, a friend I had known since I was 13/14, he bowled in the same bowling league as my dad and everyone else. Mack helped me with my homework, as I got older, we started to get closer. He would take me to dinner or the movies or hang out at his place. For a time, he was my best friend. My best friend left in the middle of the night one night after her son was buried, and the guy was sentenced and never came back. I filled that void with my guy friends; each one had a purpose with me. I was still living with Kenton, but my time there became less and less the more everyone was partying. I liked hanging out with Mack, who was much older than I was at the time. I don't know why I always went with the older guys, but I did. We had fun, and that's what counted. Everyone i hung around did something, drank, took pills, meth it didn't matter, there was always something so I was bouncing from Kenton to Mack i felt bad about the way I was treating Mack because he was so kind and so sweet, but that didn't stop me from using him to get what I wanted. I would learn just how much fun was too much fun.

CHAPTER 5

It is the summer of 2008, and I'm at Kentons but barely. When I did spend time there, I would get to know his daughter. A teenager at the time. We would have a lot of fun when she was there, which wasn't much, but when she came around, we got pretty close. I didn't know then how close we would become until the next year. Eventually, she would become more like a daughter to me, not just another teenager. She was so mature for her age and I knew that she had already been through so much at her young age. I tried to guide her down a good path while burning mine as I went on. Sometime during the previous winter or spring, I acquired a job at an auto parts store in town. I liked my job; I was learning a lot and felt like I was getting pretty good at the tasks required for that job. I had one problem, though, I was partying every night. At first, it was just my days off, but by the middle to end of the summer, I would have a phone conversation that would turn my world upside down; I had recently gotten in touch with Brendon, he called one night real late, and we were both drinking, but we talked until daybreak when we hung up, he told me he wanted to be with me again, music to my ears, but later that day I would find out that he is married and that the phone calls the night before wasn't suppose to happen, I was devastated. I immediately went to find a bottle of liquor and stayed that way for a long time every night. By this point, Kenton wasn't so fun anymore and started to get on my case about my behavior. I left his place from time to time. I would stay in hotels or find guy friends to crash with, who always required a favor in exchange for my stay. I kept my stuff hidden in the back of that auto parts store for as long as I could until I got caught by a manager and had to find somewhere else to hide it. Every night was a different scene, sometimes, I would go bar hopping and end up in sketchy situations, like the time I took off to South Carolina with Bob, a guy that I met at the alley; we knew each other from the alternative high school. It was all fun and games until we got pulled over, and he got arrested. I was told to walk home, I did just that; I walked in the pitch black night up to Sassafras mountain to my parent's house. Honestly, I was terrified the whole time and still a little screwed up. I didn't care who I was with or what happened to me. At this point in my life, I was only existing. I would disappear for days on end, at this time, unless it were a drunken phone call; my family didn't hear from me. Though I felt like I was the life of the party, I was dead inside. The drugs and alcohol had taken over my soul and I had no conscience now. I would lie, cheat, and do whatever I had to do to feed my habits. I was staying with Mack for a while, and things were getting pretty serious; he even asked me to marry him; I told him I was still single at 25 and sure I'd marry him; shortly after that conversation, the wild child in me took over, and I was gone again, not too much gone though cause he would see me every payday then once I got what i wanted, I would disappear until ed me down though, I can honestly say that he was one of the better ones in my life. I would give anything to make up for all that heartache and pain that I caused back then, what now seems like a lifetime ago. I was so wild, carefree, and bad on drugs that most nights, I couldn't tell you where or who I had been with. In August of 2008, my wild ways would ultimately cause me to simultaneously make the biggest mistake of my life and the most incredible moment in my existence. A true bittersweet moment in time. Now that I have admitted to being wild and promiscuous, it will come as no surprise that I was blacked out for several months, with very few memories of that time period. In October 2008, I was half living with a family member and on pills and meth heavy. It was always a party; I thought I was living my best life, that was until Halloween, I was at the; Iar with my group of buddies, we were all just drinking have a good time; at some point, I must have blacked out because I woke up in some guys bed that I didn't know. He told me this big story about how I got there but I thought it was bull, so I asked around and found out that I had been drugged that night. I tried to put it all out of my mind, but it wasn't easy. I chose to drown my pain into more drugs and more alcohol. I can remember plain as day the day that my life would change forever. For the past few days, I would wake up and do my normal "breakfast of champions', whatever pills I manage to score. but except this time, I wasn't getting high; that's because I would immediately get sick afterward. My family member asked me if I was pregnant. I honestly thought after losing the first one that I couldn't conceive.So I placed a call and had someone bring me a test. That test would literally change my whole world. A little chapter I like to call the miracle. I took the test, and when I said I threw it out the bathroom I threw it, it hit a mirror, I believe was in the living room. The test was positive, and I was immediately overwhelmed. Now why now, how could I have this baby? I was a monster, an addict. I made a few phone calls to a couple of the guys I remember having slept with; it was not the best conversation to have, and I got mixed emotions from them. I remember feeling so lost, so confused. I tried remembering the previous few months and placing faces and names, but I was still getting high and not thinking too straight. I remember going to the dr and confirming the at-home test results. I knew it was time to make a decision. This is what I knew; I was homeless, this time though by choice; I refused to live with my parents, I was still hooked on drugs, and I had no idea who the father of my child was. I felt like I was the worst woman on the face of the planet. The thing that trashy daytime talk shows are made of. I told my family I was expecting and did receive a lot of support from them. More than what I expected anyway, especially from my parents. I still was rebelling and refused to go home. I chose to spend the next eight months homeless, well, not any type of permanent home anyway. I would bounce from Fun Kenton to Make mainly. They both took care of me in that they made sure I ate. I slowed down a bit with the drugs during my pregnancy, but still used occasionally; looking back now, a little was too much. My time on the streets was an experience, most of the time, I would tell people about my current situation, and I was able to get them to buy me something to eat. I was going to dr regularly by this time, and it was then that I heard her heartbeat for the first time. I know at that very moment that my life had been forever changed. Fall turned to winter, though, which meant cold nights. I knew that I needed to do something to protect myself and my unborn child from the elements. Even at this new low, I refused to go home. I went to a bar one night, yes, I was drinking; I know, shame, right? I just wanted to be like everyone else having a good time so I drank, not as much i did before, but enough, i guess. Anyway I can remember arguing with some guy about something, and the altercation started to get heated when this scruffy-looking cowboy stepped in and ran the guy off. Fitz was a student at the local college I would soon find out, and he was willing to sneak me into his dorm room to sleep. I would begin a whirlwind romance with him that was so intense. I stayed with him the rest of that winter, winter 2009. We got along rather well; he would take me out to eat, or to the movies, always such a gentleman, always so sweet. Spring of 2009, I found out that I was having a baby girl. That day, I rode out to my parents place, riding with my daddy listening to the radio when a familiar song came on, "Gunpowder and Lead" by Miranda Lambert, my wee one was kicking me, and I knew she would be a fireball. I named her after Miranda and changed the spelling to make her name more unique. It wouldn't be too long until I Would have a terrifying experience. I was having major back pain during the last few months of my pregnancy and would have to take Tylenol. I tried not to do anything any stronger. I saw a doctor on friday, and he told me exactly how to take the Tylenol. I followed his instructions to the letter, but by the first part of That next week, I was sick, like an exorcist. I remember going to Singles to meet up with my mom. I didn't even make it through the door. I was rushed to the hospital and discovered that my liver enzymes had shot through the roof; essentially, I overdosed on tylenol; it had built up in my system. The nurses got me hooked up to all the machines and tried to find her heartbeat, but they could not. The worst thoughts were going through my mind; I couldn't bear to lose her too. This one nurse came in and I was telling her how frightened I was of losing her; that's when she told me "I'll be back," and brought me a variety of juices. I picked the apple one and drank it. I guess Myranda liked it because she started to move, and I could hear a strong heartbeat. I knew then that my baby girl was going to be strong, just like her mama. I was in the hospital for a few days; when I got out I learned that Fitz was angry with me about something I had nothing to do with. Up to this point, other than when I would get the wild hair, things between us were great. He bought her a little cup and a few outfits. He took me camping that spring. He was angry with me nonetheless. After a night of chasing him around town and finally spending the night outside of the college, I decided to leave that situation and at eight months pregnant, decided to finally go home, to the mountain, to my parent's house. I did better there than I thought I would. I went to child birthing classes and actually enjoyed it. Once a week, I would use those classes as an excuse to stay at Kentons house afterward. That's where all my friends were. The last couple weeks though I was home every night. My parents were very supportive of me and excited to meet their new grandbaby.she had a name now, and I was putting it on everything. I had it on her carseat, which is how my bonus daughter would find out her name. Then she told me that she would be claiming her as a sister, which meant she would always be there for her. My mom and half-sisters gave me a baby shower, i got so much for her, so I spent the rest of the month getting ready, making sure my bag was packed right, that I had the carseat right in my mom's car, any and everything I could think of to make sure I was ready for her day of arrival. I was due on July 4th, 2009. I thought that's cool. I'll have an independent baby. I would soon find out that my sweet precious daughter was anxious to get into this world. I went to a birthday party on June 20, 2009, and was told to stick my feet in the cold river water to cool off because, of course I was huge at this point and hot and miserable, so I did just that, and the next morning will always be a vivid memory in my head.

CHAPTER 6

June 21, 2009 did not start like any other Sunday normally. That morning around 5 or 6 , I awoke to a wet bed. I said, "I know I didn't pee on the bed." I got up to take a bath. I no longer sat down when the pain started. Because of the birthing classes, I was a little bit prepared or thought I was, but I wasn't prepared for how quickly everything happened. I screamed through the door to my dad to wake up Mom that I was going into labor. I live about 45 minutes from my local hospital, so calling 911 wasn't an option. She would have been born a Sassafras girl, for sure. My mom woke up and jumped into the shower to get woken up one night; she slept well, right? Anyway, while she was taking a shower, I called the birthing center at the hospital and told them I would be checking in within the hour. The lady reminded me to breathe and use what I had learned in birthing class to help me through until I could get there. Remember, Father's Day happened to fall on June 21, so my dad left to help prepare a special breakfast for my grandfather. My mom got ready, and off we went. I have never been in so much pain in my life, thank God my mom can drive the way she does. She got me to the hospital at about 8;30, 9 that morning. I was checked in and put into a room. Because it was Sunday, I had to wait for an epidural, or at least for the ones that gave it to get there. I was in pain, but I wasn't alone. My mom and my oldest half-sister held my hands, helping me breathe and stay comfortable. Finally, the epidural arrived and was administered, and honestly didn't have time to kick in before, shortly after 11 am, my daughter was born. They said she was born little, a preemie, but she was perfect. They placed her in my arms, and I knew then that I had to change my ways. I had to become a mom that she could look up to and admire. I had to be the mom that was there every night, I had to be her mom. After she returned from getting checked out and cleaned up, the nurses put her in her little incubator, and she raised her head to look around. I knew then she was going to be strong and brave. She would have to be, to be raised by me. Not long after she was born, my room began to fill up with family and friends. I will never forget my grandmother coming in and walking straight over to her to pick her up to hold her. I waited until she was sitting down and looking into the baby girl's eyes; I told her that her name was Myranda Jewel, after her great-grandmother. I chose that name to honor the woman I admire the most. I did this knowing wholeheartedly that naming her after the woman I most admired would secure her strength that I knew she was born with. The second best moment from that day was when my father held her for the first time, "his fathers Day present" To this day, I don't think I could top that one. My mother looked at her with such loving eyes; I wondered if that's how she had looked at me some 20-odd years before. When I saw that baby change our lives, I meant it. Life had become complete again. Things were still chaotic; I didn't know what I was going to do, I still wanted to hang out with my friends and party, but I wanted to be a good mom at the same time. In the beginning, after we got home from the hospital, things went well for a while. My parents went to work and I stayed home with the baby. I was very nervous around her for the first while, afraid to even give her an actual bath. I would take her to the kitchen sink to clean her up. I'm a new mom, and she did not come with a handbook. Despite the odds, I enjoyed my time with her so much, I couldn't stop watching her, admiring the perfect little girl that I created. I still didn't know who the other half of her was, and honestly, I didn't care. She was mine, and that's all that mattered. I stayed with my parents for over a month, I guess, before I started to get that itch to leave. I had been doing so well with everything, but I was still seeking something out there; I just couldn't put my finger on what I needed or was missing. I would find that later on down the road. It was during this time to that I needed to make a decision, I had the facts, i didn't have a stable home, not of my own, no job, and was still wild and carefree, and i knew that I could not and would not have my baby around the crowd that i was hanging out with. One day after a long discussion and serious thinking, I let my parents raise her for the first five years, just until I got my life on track. I would remain in her life during that time on and off, making the best of each visit. Though I had discussed this decision with my parents and knew I was making it right, they became public enemy number one. I would use that situation to justify getting high and then get mad at them if they wouldn't let me see her. I was beyond delusional at that time. I look back now and just think about the million other ways I could have handled that situation, but at the time, what I did seemed right. One night, things began to heat up between my mother and me, and I had the mindset of a teenager. I just wanted to have fun, let loose, be wild and free again. We argued for a time, and then, I would make one of the biggest mistakes of my life; I would call some friends and leave sassafras, walking out on my baby girl. That is one choice I will forever regret. Though things are much different now, I look back on the mistakes I made back then in shame. That night I would meet someone who would change my life forever. It's what I like to call a series of unfortunate events.

CHAPTER 7

At the end of the summer 209, I left my parent's house, leaving behind my 1-month-old daughter with my parents to go chase that high that I always craved. I hated every inch of myself for walking away, but the beast inside needed to be fed. The night I left the mountain, I walked down the road to meet some friends who would pick me up and take me to the spot where I would have a series of unfortunate events. . it began like this: I was sitting on the porch of Kentons' house when this young, good looking guy walked up. He was younger than me by a couple of years, but instantly I was smitten. I couldn't believe he told me i was pretty; I mean i was in sweats, hair pulled back, I'd been crying since I walked out of moms. He asked me if I wanted to go for a walk. I like to think of it as a walk to remember because that moment transformed my heart in ways that I, for once, did not have the words for. After that night, we spent every chance we could work together. I would try to stay with mom here and there and be with my daughter, but it was with Buck when I would stay in town. He had a place of his own, I'd stay with him, and we would talk, I told him everything, and really opened up to him, something that I didn't know was even possible for me. I told him I had a drug problem, because it's not like it wasn't obvious. He took it upon himself to help me escape those just contributing to my habits. He then became my worst enemy, but by this point, after a month or so, I was in love. We had about a month of bliss until i would screw up and lie to him about what I was getting from Kenton. He couldn't stand the young buck so from there on, it was a fight, nothing too violent; the only victim that night was a milk jug that got thrown because that was my excuse for going out to meet Kenton. My friends hated him, and he felt the same. I was torn, but I chose him. He was funny and interesting and everything I needed at that time. I knew he had the same mental issues, but I truly thought that we would fix each other. By the end of September, things with me had gotten out of hand; we agreed to seek treatment for our mental health and stay on our meds together. There was a problem with that, the meds were strong, and we were abusing them. In time we would get kicked out of hotels, miss court dates, and we had no clue what day of the week it was. All we knew was that we were in love and having fun. I have no idea how the conversation got started or who it was started with, but by the end of September, I would be in a Shelter for Women in SC. I was told it was a rehab for women, but it was a shelter for women down on their luck. My parents took me, and I still remember seeing the tear roll down my father's cheek as he told me he just wanted me to get better so I could be a baby girl's mom. I spent the whole month of October there. At first I wouldn't say I liked it, they took my phone from me, and at that time, I had to be with him. Buck had my heart. The ladies there wanted me to get closer to myself than him so they took my phone and I was left to survive. I would find out that it wasn't too hard; I made friends with the ladies there, and being sober for the first time since I was 14 felt hella good. I had some positivity there and started to get a whole new outlook on everything when one night, some of the women yelled for me through the hallway, he was there; he had driven all the way down there to get to look at me possibly, he knew we couldn't exactly talk. I was impressed; I mean, I had a guy walk to see me in a pretty good way a couple of times, but nothing like this. He did love me, I thought. There was so much to process, I mean, I was leaving the shelter in just a couple of days. Where would I go? I had 30 days to clean when I got back to that small town. The first thing I did was go to Kenton's house. I was happy, sober, and felt great. I remember having a conversation with him, and then suddenly, I went into my first seizure episode. Seizures are something that, until that point, I had never had an issue with, and would plague me for years to come. After coming out of it, though, Buck arrived in town and straight to his side, I went. We would spend the next while going from hotels to my parents house until we finally moved in with them and baby girl; it was getting colder so that's what we did. He worked with my dad or would walk from out there on sassafras to town and look for work. That's one thing I can say about Buck; he was a worker. For a while, everything seemed almost perfect. Though my parents lost our home because of the financial disasters of 2008, we moved into a smaller trailer and did our best to turn it into a home. All that would shatter before Christmas 2009, I was hit with the earth shattering news that Buck had been locked up. I say earth-shattering because I had just got him back, we were happy. He would spend three to four months in the county jail; I would write to him daily and see him whenever I could. I even walked in the snow to see him a few times. I was so miserable to begin with, and upset because I never knew he was doing anything wrong. my parents moved off Sassafras mountain. I was sad to say goodbye to my childhood home, but after everything there, it was time to say goodbye. My parents would find a cute place not too far from town, and I would move in with them and Myranda. When we left the mountain, she was getting big now, about 7-8 months old. We got settled into the new place, my parents both were working, so I got to spend time alone with the baby girl. I loved it.we had our own little routine of toons, naps, and snacks. I enrolled in school for the first time. I enjoy school more now that I am older than I ever did in high school. My life seemed to fall into place for the first time. I was still going out with my friends, but not until my parents were home, and I always tried to go back home; some nights I didn't though. I was in my routine for a while, until I got a phone call. Buck is out and wants to talk. I tell you, in that instant, all those months of hard work just went all to hell. I gave in, and there would begin something that to this day will be referred to as never over. It all started from something he sent me while in jail, and it said no matter what our circumstances were, that what was never over. It became our pact, and we would need it to survive each other that next year. In April 2010, I got married again. This one was different; I remembered it. I will never forget slow dancing in the kitchen to our wedding song, but I knew at that moment I had found my one, I didn't care if he just got out of jail, hell I had a record, what mattered was that he understood me, he was there for me. He rented a room in the same house where I lived with Jamie. After we were married, I was allowed to live with him, the landlords were conservative. The first few weeks were great. At one point, he and I would move back in with my parents. He had a job, he and I were going to church together, something we started at the old place, things were going well; we were baptized together, my parents let me take the baby girl to church a few times; I thought things were great. Little did I know another bomb was about to be dropped in my lap. I'm sitting with my mom, and I think I was even taking a nap with Myranda or watching tv with her when I got a message from him. This man tells me he was hurt at work and going to the hospital for something he got in his eye, "ok ill be right there," I said. Well, before I could leave, my phone would ring again; this time, it was his boss on the other line informing me that Buck was headed to the county jail, not the hospital. At this moment, my head is just spinning. He's been with me when he's not at work, how is he in trouble? Come to find out, he was living a whole different life than the one that we had together. Once again, he's back in jail and I'm left to pick up the pieces of my shattered heart; we had been married a whole month. I pretty well stayed at moms while he was there. I'd go out on occasion and party, and yes, I'll admit it, that paycheck he was supposed to receive, well, I was supposed to bail him out with it; I chose to buy drinks at the alley till the money ran out. All my friends thanked him for that night. I didn't care. This made twice that he played me for a damn fool. I was out for revenge in any way I could get it. I did not care what situation I put myself in as long as it would get back to him and I could make him hate me back. I have never felt like this before, this intense hate for someone, but I still have this burning passion for him that is just as intense. I tried to forget him for the most part and move on. I was addicted to him, though, and after spending all day in the courtroom, I was told he was being released, I remember high-stepping it all the way to the jail. They popped the doors, and in his arms, I was. What can i say, it was convict love, but a love only experienced once in life. This is the love that I will soon learn from. Learn how to survive. Upon his release, he was told by my parents that he was no longer welcome at their house. He always managed to make a way, he was smart and had a way with words, and he always figured out a way of keeping us a roof. We would end up in a camper at Macks for the remainder of that summer. That year, though we had nothing, Buck made my birthday special. He spoiled me with one of my favorite dishes every night that week. No one has ever put that much effort into me before. I remember going to get high that night afterward and I left him, but I did that a lot; I would just take off; that monkey had a strong hold on my back. I can't blame him for what was to come. Afterward, I returned to rehab or a mental institution for a few days. That was our thing, he would go to jail, then me in rehab or mental institutions. That's when I would discover that I suffer from PTSD, big surprise there, and multiple personality disorder. Early that fall, he went back to jail. When he got out this time, he worked everything out to where we both were getting a ticket out of there. A fresh start is what we told ourselves. We moved 3 hours from my hometown, down east to Greensboro. I have never been that far away before. I was excited and terrified. I signed something with my parents that would protect my daughter so that they could legally take care of her. I knew that I had made the right decision, but doing so just made me feel like the scum of the earth. I had walked away from her again. I tried to push through the pain and he assured me everything would be ok. We get there, and well, let's say that's when the hell began. It didn't take long before we got odd jobs here and there and even managed to score a car; it was older but a way of going. Summer turned to fall. I saw Myranda for Halloween, which made me happy. Thanksgiving, I never felt more alone and would get drunk; that was my normal anyway. I hated being there, hated him, hated myself for leaving my daughter, and I stayed drunk. As fall turned to winter, I knew I had to find a way home for Christmas. Through sacrifices and a favor for a favor, I could make it. Myranda must have known it, too, because when I got there, she was standing in the window jumping up and down. I had a great visit but when I got back to my apartment, let me tell you, how either of us made it out of that apartment alive, I will never know. We were drinking nightly, and every night was another fight. By this point, almost every fight was physical. He knew he had a problem, I knew I had a problem, and I even checked into a hospital, but the fact was one of us had to get out. That time would come shortly after Valentine's Day that year. I was happy to see him go back to jail that time; he had really hurt me a couple nights before, I had a way out, but I lied and said nothing happened. Once he was gone I had a decision to make. I knew I could not make it there alone; I was already having horrible luck, so I called the person who took me back to my apartment after he was sentenced and told them I wanted to return home. It would be a while before I saw him again. Of course, when I did finally see him, it was not like picking up where we left off; this time was different . It seemed like every time he would go to jail, a piece of him would be missing when he got out. He was colder, and we were both getting high daily. A lot of that summer is a blur; there was a lot of fighting that I do know. One night I thought we were going to kill each other, it got so bad he was driving up and down the road at high speed, so I hid behind a truck and called the cops. I would take him back when he got out. Our marriage had turned into a nightmare. We had turned into a nightmare. I was everything I could be and so was he just to put up with back into rehab and get clean. The next thing I remember is briefly laying on the ground as the ambulance was getting me. I heard them say I was gone at one point but ended up in the ICU. I would find out later that he tried to kill me. I have nightmares any time I have to stay in them. I would see Myranda mainly when he was in jail, because I didn't want her around all the destruction we were causing. At some point, we had managed to work things out long enough to rent a room from this sweet old lady. There things were a little better. We would go back down east together one last time; that would be our best time together yet. He had court, and we were nervous the whole way, planning a strategy in case he went to jail and I was left stranded. Court went well and for the first time in a long time, we felt free, more than we had in our apartment, more than ever. He took me on a surprise detour, and we went to the infamous town on which the show Mayberry is based. To this day, when my life gets chaotic, I'll tell myself that I need a Mayberry stay of mind. It was a whole level of peace that I had not found anywhere else. On the way home, we took the parkway back; it was incredible. Between the state lines, I took a picture of one leg in NC and one leg in Va, just like in my favorite movie, A Walk To Remember. I took it so that i can say I've been in two places at the same time. When we returned to the house where we were renting a room, things were peaceful for a while. As usual, peace wouldn't last long, and he would go back to jail, 3 hours away. Would you believe I begged for a ride to go get him? I did, though, and that night, I saw the devil in his eyes and things were never the same. He had put my initials on him; I have no clue why, but he did. We were going to this recovery place in town, deep down, we both wanted to get better. I enjoyed the place; I could be me there and so could he; the problem was, we were making friends with people that we should not have been making friends with, they had pills, so instantly, we let go of anything close to living a sober life and go through the next few weeks in a pill-induced haze. Somehow, I have his initials on me, I haven't covered them up because they serve as a reminder that I am a survivor; I did cheat death and a reminder of what never to tolerate again. I don't remember much but I do remember that we were at somebody's house that we had been staying at, and I told him that I wanted to go to the hospital so that he would come in and finish the job. I managed to get myself released so that I could go and find him. I did all right, and the fight was on; I was furious at him; after everything we had been through, how could he do this to me. At some point, one of the nice ladies that works there came outside to break us up, and I told her I was going to take her out, I did not mean out to coffee or breakfast. Eventually, the police were called, and I was taken back to the ICU. I still had many drugs in my system from the night before. I was in the hospital for a few days when this counselor came into my room and told me I was going to a state hospital. No, I don't think so; I asked for a second option as I threw the book at him. My option was jail so I could lay my head at the county jail for nine days. When I got out, Myranda sat on the counter playing with the nice police officers. Seeing her made me realize that my life was nothing compared to the one I was about to live. With that, other than our final court date together and beyond a conversation from time to time, I have closed that chapter of unfortunate events. Through the years, I have had time to work through the anger and pain, and I forgive him for everything; after all, I wasn't exactly innocent. The experience changed me. I can say that much. By this time, I had survived two abusive marriages and several sexual assaults. I took a stand and swore never again would I allow anyone to lay hands on me that wished to harm me. I built a wall around my heart, the pain was intense, and I needed to protect myself. Buck was going to prison, and I was free for the first time since laying eyes on him. Then, the phoenix within me began to rise, and I would start finding myself and healing my heart and soul.

CHAPTER 8

In spring 2011, I said goodbye to city life one last time. I made the 3 1/2 trip back home to that small town with which I had a love/hate relationship. I moved back in with my parents and Myranda. She was close to 2 years old then, and I was enjoying every moment I could with her. My mom had enrolled her in classes for socialization. I was encouraged to participate, and that was our special time together, we would play games in that little classroom or on the playground. I must say that I was happy at that point in my life. All I ever wanted was to be a good mom to Myranda. I would stay with them for a while, through the summer and most of the fall; before that itch would get the better of me and I would leave once again. I would reconnect with a guy I had dated for a very short time in middle school. Alex, he drank, but that was it, i had managed to get my hands on pills behind his back, which would cause issues between us. They had such pills on me that it's like I merely existed to get high. The only time I was truly sober was when my mom agreed to let me have Myranda while she worked through the week. I enjoyed my time with her, she could walk well by then, and we would play outside, or I would invent games to play inside. I am complete when she is with me; I am happy, and I truly want to be my best for her. The weekends were a different story, I would drop her off at mom on Fridays, I and Alex would go to a party, and by the end of the night, we would be arguing. That should have been my first sign that things wouldn't work out between us, I was always disappearing on him. He would go inside a store, and I would be gone before he got back and disappear for days. I would call my best friend Maryanne and tell her to make up an excuse to get me. I really didn't even like Alex; I stayed because it was just something to do. New Year's Eve 2012 is a nightmare that is etched in my memories. He and I were at a friend's house, drinking as usual. I was drinking heavily that night, but at some point, I decided to go and lay down on the couch upstairs. I was awakened by my pants being taken off of me and I was assaulted once again. I got the guy off of me and ran downstairs to where the guy I was lying passed out. I tried to wake him up and tell him what happened to me, but my efforts were useless. I looked around the room; I wasn't going to let him get away with this; damn it, i'd been assaulted too many times in my life, so I looked around the room and there on the table was a knife, something snapped in me, I ran up the stairs, I was going to kill him, in those moments, everything that had happened since I was at camp that last year just came flooding back, I went into his room where he was just laying there passed out like he hadn't done anything at all just 10-15 min before that. I took that knife and was going to slit his throat, but as I got into the motions to finish him off, the guy who owned the house came in and tried to stop me. Instead of cutting the guy who had just assaulted me, I cut a huge gash in my arm. After that, i broke down, I was bleeding pretty badly and the guy who saved me, I guess, literally took me out of the room with my arm in his mouth, holding pressure on the wound until he could get me cleaned up. I told him what happened to me, and he helped me wake up my fellow to tell him. We must have left shortly after that because I remember getting stitches and returning to my fellows house. We argued the whole time, he kept making me repeat what had happened to me, then finally left. I thought he would kick the guy's ass or something, but no, he went over there to drink with them. I tell you, I felt betrayed then. I stayed at his house for a long time till his dad showed up and gave me a ride to my parents. I told my mom what happened to me, and of course like all the other times, I wasn't listened to. In February of 2012, I had court against Buck, he was being sentenced to prison and I jumped at the chance to ask the judge for a divorce. I need to be free from him and that disaster we called a marriage. A few weeks later, a knock on my mom's front door would make me one happy woman, it was a police officer, and he had my divorce papers. I'm not kidding when I say I hugged the officer's neck; he said, 'I never had anyone hug me over divorce papers before,' I replied with, "You must not know who my ex-husband is then." I wanted to celebrate my new found freedom, so I went out and about. This would begin a few months of chaos in my life; after everything I had gone through, I just wanted to have fun. Maryanne would call me her "free bird," and I was; I just floated from here to there. I was staying with a girlfriend for a little while, didn't really date anyone in particular, I was still talking to Alex, mostly when I would get drunk, and I had reconnected with a Brendon for some reason. This one night, I had been talking to both of them, while drinking, not something I recommend. I was supposed to meet up with Brendon, but when I woke up the next morning, Brendon was not who I was with, I ended up with the other one, Alex. I woke up, realized I made a mistake, called Maryanne and was like, "I have a problem, I got Alex and Brendon mixed up" She laughed at my predicament and said, "Well where ya at, and I'll send your cousin to pick you up," I was like "Alexes" with that tiny voice of shame. He was in the shower, but he heard me leaving and ask, "What ya doing," I was like, "Leaving, this wasn't supposed to have happened," and with that, I left, going to my cousin's house, it wouldn't take long until he would come up there to get me to "talk," my cousin being the horses ass that he is, gave that fool a bottle of liquor to drink before we talked, little did I know that that bottle of liquor held a key within it, a key that would open up new doors later on down the road and ultimately bring me to where and who I am today. Anyway, I went on a ride with Alex to talk, yeah, right, this guy took me to the top of some damn mountain; I had no clue where I was, we talked for a minute, and then he passed out. I mean, out cold, I text my cousin with what little service I had to say I was going to kick his ass for this. Four hours later, he woke up and took me back to my cousin's place. That was the last time I would have any dealings with him. I returned to my parents house for a little while until I started staying with Bridgette, one of my girlfriends. It is at her place where I would shoot up for the first time. That high was unlike anything I had ever experienced before. I did it that once, but that feeling will forever be sketched into me. I didn't stay there long, after leaving her place, I found myself staying at the homeless shelter in town. There I would meet a few new friends and be somewhat productive for a short time. I had started slowly going back to classes at the recovery center. I had talked to that nice lady who I "threatened to take out," and all was forgiven. I remained on good behavior for a while, but one night, I would throw it all away. I took off with some friends one night to have some fun. I guess we were out past curfew because the next day, I was asked to leave. Back to my parents, I go once again. This time though, my dad told me I needed to get a job. I knew I needed to do something with my life, but I wasn't ready to take that first step. I was enjoying spending time with the baby girl. One night, I received an unexpected message from Fitz, the guy from the college. Anyway, he was in town and wanted to talk. I, of course, said ok, he said he wanted to get me out of Nc and take me out west. He thought that getting me away from my surroundings would be a better life for me. I knew that I couldn't and wouldnt bring Myranda with me, and i also knew that i was not going to make that mistake twice in one lifetime, so I asked him to run me to a friend's house real quick, i scored some coke, just enough to prove a point, I finished with my lines then got back in the truck. He wasn't stupid, he knew what i had done, but with the harshest coldest voice possible, I told him that leaving with him would never be an option, and with that I went home. I landed a job at a pizza place in town a few days later and worked for a few weeks, Mothers day weekend 2012, I spent the weekend with Brendon. Yeah, I know you would think I would have learned, right? I was there all weekend, missing work, which got me fired, but I was there. We had always had a drinking problem when we were together, so it was no surprise when I got drunk and yelled at him about how much I hated him for what he did to me. He thought that after I got it all out and we talked that everything would be ok, that I would give him another chance, after that much hell, hell no, it was time for him to have a broken heart, so i called a friend and disappeared. I would see him one last time in my mother's driveway, I had left my id of everything at his place. He gave me a choice then and there, and I chose to walk away from him one last time. About a week after that, i would visit my ob-gyn and discuss birth control options, i had trouble with a lot of the common methods, so here I was in his office talking about my options, i told him I wanted to tie my tubes, i had made a deal with young buck that I wouldn't have kids anymore, i know stupid right, but dammit he still had a hold on me. Anyway, the doctor and I are conversing about getting my tubes tied, and he asks me, "So what will you do if you meet a guy who wants to have children?"I responded, "Maybe I'll meet one that already has children ', how true that would become soon enough. I guess it was either that day or maybe the next, but by the end of the week, I would call Maryanne to pick me up. She informed me that she was watching these three kids of a friend of hers, but she didn't care to get me once their dad got there. I had no idea that that trip to a place called Sapphire would ultimately transform my entire existence, and that I would meet and fall in love with one of the most incredible men I have ever met. The next morning, I would wake up at her house, and my world would forever be changed. Starting a new chapter in my story.

CHAPTER 9

In May of 2012, I was at a good friend's house; I called her the day before to come to get me from my mom's place; I needed a break. Anyway, I woke up the next morning to not just her three kids running around but three other little kids I never saw before. I asked her, "Who are those?" she replied, "Remember, I told you I was babysitting for Eric ", "oh yeah, guess I forgot." I spent the day watching all the kids play and thinking about life. I knew in my heart of hearts that I needed a change. I needed to get clean; I needed stability. That afternoon, Eric, the father of the children, would show up to pick his kids up. By then, I had made friends with the cute little redhead boy Zack, not even two at the time, as well as this adorable little girl Gracie, age six at the time. I guess we were friends by the end of the day because she gave me a friendship bracelet and invited me to dinner that night with her, her dad, and her brothers. I accepted, not knowing how one meal would change my whole existence. The first thing I learned about this man was that he could cook. He fixed this mouth watering dish of chicken divine; to this day it's one of my favorites. I admired how he was with his children, he gave them all so much attention; honestly, i never saw anything like it before. I only had one child, and she was a handful and the age of 2, and here he was juggling 3 like it was just another thing, I was impressed. He put them to bed and then he and I talked. I told him a little about my past and current situation, and he was so understanding, unlike anything I had ever experienced. I felt safe there; I felt something that I was unfamiliar with. I spent the night and well, the rest is history. In this part of my story, to tell it truthfully, I first need to break it in half. After that first initial night, I ended up spending more and more time with him. He co-parented with his children's mother April, which allowed us to get to know one another. I would learn that that bottle of liquor my horse's ass of a cousin gave to Alex belonged to him. To begin with, I would stay with my parents now and then, and he would come hang out with me after work. One night my dad told me, "If you can't stay away from him, then just move in with him ", I took his wonderful fatherly advice and moved in with him. We had only been hanging out for a couple of weeks. During that time, in May 2012, I had my tubes tied. I had no problem with that decision since I didn't plan on having any more children. A couple days before my daughter's birthday, he ran in and told me my father had been taken to the hospital; he was having chest pains.I met my mom at the hospital, and she informed me that he was ok, but they would keep him overnight. She wanted me to stay with myranda at their house and ensure she got to daycare the next morning.Eric stayed with me that night at my parent's house, sleeping in the living room so I could sleep next to Myranda, and I remember thinking, "This guy is something; he has a heart" to this point, I knew very few people with a heart. My daughter's birthday came and went, my dad came home from the hospital, and everything seemed ok for a bit. Due to unfortunate circumstances, he did not get to see his children too much after that day. We spent the rest of the summer getting to know one another. In August 2012, I came to a "moment of awakening" you see, i wasn't clean when I met Eric; I knew i wanted to get clean, but getting my mind and heart to receive the same message at the same time was damn near impossible. Not long after we met, I went out of state with him to work and left on day two in the middle of the night. I literally called Kenton to get me. In a way, that was the first wake up call. The second was that in a short time, I lost at least a handful or more of friends to various things. For a while, I would keep going through the addiction cycle, that revolving door that addiction creates. I would get a tattoo that I don't remember and end up in sticky situations where Eric would have to save me. I admit that first summer, I put him through hell. At the end of the summer, I would receive a letter from my ex husband Buck. That letter sent me into this tornado of emotions. He told me that if I wanted to try again to meet him at the bus station. For a whole 48 hours, I battled with the idea. I was afraid that if I met him, he would kill me, i was afraid that i would never see my daughter again, but for every fear, there was this other voice telling me that he was my soulmate, and maybe he was changed. I told Eric about everything, probably much more than he wanted to know, it was enough for him to stay out of work for a few days to make sure I didn't make that potentially fatal mistake. That day arrived, the day I was supposed to meet him at the bus station. I remember being on my knees, my head in Eric's lap, bawling my eyes out. Then and there, I would have that "moment of awakening" that I needed to become who I am today. That night, the new guy took me to a bridge that was pretty close to where we were living.

Once I got to the edge of that bridge, I took off that damn ring that became more like a damn handcuff, and I slung the damn thing as far as I could into the river. For a time, I would be done with him. After that, Eric and I rode around so I could get some music therapy out of my system. I can't really sing for shit, but I feel good doing it. I am able to release the pain that resides in the core of my soul. After that night, we just spent every moment we could together. I was falling in love, I kinda fell in love the first night, shhh don't tell him though. After all, a girl has to protect her reputation. My birthday, September 7, 2012, is a day I will forever be grateful for, my clean date. A few days before, I received a phone call from my mom saying that my daughter was experiencing some issues after having some tubes put in her ears. I went to moms right; right before I got the call, I was getting high with a buddy.The moment I walked in the door of my mother's, I felt like the lowest person in the world. My baby girl needed me, and i was too fucked up to know what was wrong with her. She had tubes in her ears in 2011 and again in 2012; 2012 just a day after the tubes were put in her ears, her eyes began to cross. She was three at the time. We would get the problem with her eyes fixed via eye surgery within that year or so, before she started kindergarten. I told Eric I was messed up when my mom called me about Myranda. He gave me one choice, "family, or drugs' '. For once in my life, I chose family. At this point, all the drugs ever gave me was an empty soul. On my birthday, I had made that conscious decision that I was completely done with drugs and alcohol. For the next several months, I would attend recovery classes, when I asked for forgiveness and to come back, I told the ladies that I was making a heartfelt attempt at my recovery. There were things I struggled with in the beginning, like the idea of a higher power, and owning up to my mistakes and flaws, asking for forgiveness. Someone told me once, "You can turn anything into a higher power, even the moon.", "even the moon?" i replied, somewhat confused because i thought it had to be religiously based and I want to that point yet. I chose the moon as my guiding force. I would go for a ride and just stare, hoping it could read my thoughts. Many nights I would go outside and let go of all my secrets, I felt as though the moon heard every word. In October 2012, I married that sweet, sexy man that saved my life. Marriage number 4 (if we count viva las Severrville), this marriage would be different. This man was a different breed, he had one of the best hearts I have ever seen in anyone and the most patience I have ever seen in anyone. October would bring several changes into my life. The first was the marriage, the second was that his kids all moved in with us. That was an adventure; I went from being around none or one to having three wild rugrats around me. His middle son and I were already having a rocky start, he locked me out of the house one day after he got home from school. I knew I had my work cut out for me. That first Halloween with them was great, we didn't have the money extra to go all out for costumes, but we did the best we could with homemade ones. It was nice having a little family. One night I decided to get an attitude with my wonderful new husband. Instead of hitting or screaming at me, he kinda held me by my shoulders, walking me backwards out the front door. My reaction oh my gosh, I couldn't believe that somebody would be this mean, i was in shorts, and it was like 40 outside. He told me that I could stay out until I "cooled off". I did not lose my attitude as a matter of fact; if anything I was just shocked for a good bit. I got cold eventually and got him to let me in and to this day, pick and choose what season I wish to fight in. I saw he was a different breed, but I was unsure if i liked it. The holidays came and went, and a new year dawned. I continued to go to the recovery classes, and even received my 90 days clean chip from NA. I would pick up my daughter from my parents on the weekends; she immediately took up with the other kids. Finally, we were going to be a family; I was hoping that that would be enough to keep me sober. Those first three years flew by and in that time, we would move off one mountain and into a valley. We had acquired our own trailer. Things were great in the beginning of this new situation; we fixed up all the rooms and made it our home. During that time, i had written a poem entitled "a mothers Love", published in a multi author book. All I ever wanted was a chance with my baby girl. Prayers would be answered though, in 2015. I had been in the trailer for about a year when another change happened; my daughter moved in with us. I wish I could say it had been under different circumstances, but she was sick with Mono, my mom couldn't get the time off work, so my dad told me to take her home and care for her. It was a bittersweet moment because I made that 5-year mark I told them. I got my shit together in 5 years, and the feelings of fulfillment hit me. We were one family at last. This is when I started to step it up in the house. I cooked and constantly ensured our house was clean, but I had a little secret for my daily energy; I was taking my oldest stepsons ADHD medication. On weekends we would take the kids and have fun, walking was our favorite thing to do, and going to the lake. We fell into our little routine, Eric worked, the kids at school, and I stayed home. Because of the seizures, I can not legally drive, nor do I know how. I was never really taught, That should be obvious since I wrecked the first time I tried to drive independently. So no job, no license leaves me at home. I cleaned, I talked to friends on the phone, by then, I had gotten back in connection with my best friend Amber from my teen years and watched tv. I felt like I was on autopilot. Every day that passes, I feel my depression getting worse and worse. I finally voiced my concerns to my husband who got me a job with him and his dad. His dad owned a landscaping business. There I would learn many different things, and the techniques used for different things. This seemed to work for me, I had my own money, spent more time with the man I was head over heels in love with, and finally, I was happy and content. At the beginning of the summer 2014, I went out of work to have a partial hysterectomy, BAD MISTAKE, in the coming years, I would regret the decision. When I came home from the hospital, my mother-in-law came up every day to sit with me to make sure I would behave myself; by then everyone knew how stubborn I was. I have prescribed pain pills afterward; everyone thought that since i had a few years of clean time that i would be ok. That is far from the truth, let me explain, for a year now, I was sneaking into my stepson's ADHD medicine because to some people, it speeds them up, I was one of those people. I enjoyed having the energy to be the "super-mom" I was trying to be. When I started taking the pills the doctor prescribed me after the hysterectomy, I felt myself slipping back into that dark place. I played it off to everyone like it wasnt even happening, but the whole house knew something wasn't right. I would freak out over any little thing and scream at everyone.I had turned into a monster. I found my ex husband and made a game of making his life a living hell to the point that I showed a judge a fake GPS location to have my ex husband arrested . I said he was en route to kill me and "tracked his GPS via cell number." It showed him moving, too; it was convincing enough that the judge issued a warrant for his arrest. Just because I hated him. He lives over 3 hours away, by the way. It was also about this time that I was having terrible seizure episodes. I would find out that they were PTSD induced, go figure, right? They took over my life, though and at one point, we brought someone in to help with the house and kids because the new meds that I was prescribed made me sleep all the time. I don't remember much from those few months other than getting arrested for assaulting my husband with a hairbrush and reconnecting with a close family member. In my defense, I thought my child was screaming because she was hurt, not because Eric was trying to get her to eat her veggies, and I snapped. I began to beat him with my fist until we made it to our room, then he shoved me onto the bed to get me off of him. That's when I grabbed the brush and beat him with everything I had. At that moment, I was releasing everything, all that had been done to me since I was 11 was coming out. After spending a night in jail, I called his mom to get me and she and I had gotten close those past few years. I leaned on her a lot for support. Time would pass and we would work everything out; we laugh about the hairbrush incident, and to this blur, I was abusing all my meds by this time. I didn't consider it a relapse because I wasn't on street drugs, just my own.2016, I returned to work with my husband; I was doing well too. I learned a lot about arboriculture with him and his dad. I also learned how to lay block and landscape. We were almost to the end of our season when one day if someone saw one in my hands, it was "Oh no, you better watch it; she's got her weapon out". That was the last time I would get physical with him. I would get better, though and all would go back to normal until one day, my phone rang, and I heard the most devastating news in a long time that a really close family member I had just reconnected with was now deceased. I can remember throwing down my phone and running in our bathroom; my heart was shattered, my husband came in and I told him, he was just as devastated by the news because they were best friends. The next few months were another unfortunate event that would occur; this time my nose is the victim. My husband cut a limb and it bounced back hitting my nose. I admit it was my fault; I misjudged a few things, resulting in this ugly gash in my nose. I needed stitches, of course and was rushed to a local doctors office, where I met a sweet, funny lady who stitched me right up, and told me, "You're tougher than some men i've seen in here", with this laugh that just filled the room. I have prescribed pain meds and referred to another doctor who would "give me a good nose job". I have to admit, he did a good job, there is still a small scar there still, but i'm sure not near as bad as it could have been. After the procedure, I was prescribed pain meds again and again. I didn't think that it was a big deal, nothing was going up my nose this time. During that recovery, I stayed home regularly, feeling useless because I couldn't do anything and we were struggling. Very quickly

I slid into a dark depression. By the spring of the next year, I decided that I had an easy solution to all my problems. I visited that sweet doctor who patched up my nose and had a little chit chat. I told her that I was hurting literally everywhere and that I couldn't function most days, which wasn't a lie, i have fibromyalgia found out in 2004 at the age of 18, every day is different. I told her everything through everything but my past with addiction. I'm sure she saw it in my records, but I didn't say anything. I managed to talk her into letting me join pain management. Finally I thought, the jackpot, I can get my script, not worry about it, and still stay clean. That's not exactly how things went; well, in the beginning yes, my husband trusted me with my meds, believing when I said that I wouldn't abuse them. Then I started to screw up; I ran out early one month, then another month, and that's when he made me hand them over, and called my doctor. From that moment on, he became my number 1 enemy. It became a cat-and-mouse game; he would hide them, I would find them, if i didn't, it wasn't a pleasant scene. He would leave my daily dose three and that was it. I learned to make do with that, especially since my nose worked again. It was getting wintertime, and I was saying messed up on my meds daily. I had lost hope again; my willpower, that driving force I had initially. I was always screaming at the kids; it didn't matter what for. For those years, I was a hypocrite and I was a monster. I was a hypocrite because I spoke at a recovery event, yes, I had years sober, but I was also abusing my medications. That speaking engagement would lead to writing an article for the local paper. Being Loved is the Greatest Love of All was the name of it. I wrote it hoping I would inspire others, but how can I inspire others when I'm still in the trenches?That would lead to my portrait being drawn for a project called "My Name Is", I started a relationship with a friend from high school, he was sweet, shy, and he didn't mind my habit. My husband and I were arguing all the time. I lost his trust, a hard pill to swallow, even for me. I would invite my friend over the next few months while the hubby was at work. Nothing happened then, just a conversation, but I felt a connection with him; I'd soon learn why. By spring of that year, 2017, we were almost inseparable and my husband started getting suspicious, especially when I invited him to eat Easter dinner with all of us. It wasn't too long after that I would end up almost making a huge mistake. I left one night and went to my friend's house. I wasn't thinking straight, all I knew was in my mind that I was being controlled. I spent the night there and that's when I would make a huge mistake. The next morning it was like somebody knocked the crap out of the back of my head because I sat up, looked at my surroundings, and decided that is not where I need to be. After a very long discussion with the mother of my sweet friend, and my husband, I went back home. Eric forgave me for my indiscretion and we agreed to start over. He also told me that nobody could replace the one I lost; I guess I was trying to fill that void. He and I were so close, and a piece of me died that day. I went back to work with him after that,I needed to be away from the house. I told the doctor the truth about me conning her for pills, and once again, I picked myself up from the depths of my own hell and pushed forward. As I said, I didn't really consider what I had done to be a relapse because they came from a doctor; I just picked right back up where I left off in my sobriety journey. I would go to the beach with a girlfriend in 2018 and have one more good eye opening experience, I was walking up the steps to my room, and this guy ask me for a cigarette; I tossed one down, the next thing he wanted was lighter, so i walked that down, didn't throat, he pushed me away want to break a windshield. We stood and chatted a moment, then he put his hand up my dress, then tried to pull me into the car, immediately something took over me, and I grabbed a knife I had in my bag that a awesome guy I used to know gave me when I arrived in Mississippi, and I held it up close to his then he slammed his door and sped off, I figure hell my best defense was to be the crazy white girl. As soon as I got into my room, I phoned my husband. I also decided that never again would I let anyone else touch me unless I wanted them to. I had had enough of being abused by men. I went back home and tried to forget it ever happened. It was then that i told myself NEVER AGAIN, never again will a man inappropriately touch me; this time, I would mean it.

CHAPTER 10

May 2019 will go down in my story as one of the happiest times of my life, my bonus granddaughter was born. I held her and told her I would always have her back and love her. Just another reason to want to live a better life. It was also time to get back on my psych meds, when I take them like I am supposed to, I am less likely to act out and do things that I know better than to do. On the meds, I am stable enough to function like a normal human being. After going on vacation with my family at the end of the summer of 2019, I decided that I would embark on a new adventure. You see, my husband started a tree business the year before. I was already contributing through advertising and doing secretary work. Still, I wanted to do more and after a lengthy conversation with my husband, I enrolled in Penn Foster Career College. When I started, I found the tasks challenging. It had been a while since I was in school and college was so much different than high school, even online. I did buckle down, though, and gave it my all for the next few months, bad thing was, I started to isolate myself from everyone in my life. I would soon regret this. 2020 would arrive and change everything for my little family. We would experience several losses in a short time span. The first is my grandmother, the woman my daughter carries her middle name. Death is never easy, even when it's expected. I love that woman, she was a hero to me, always so strong. I confided with her about so much, and she would either have a good story to tell me or some great advice. Her passing broke my heart. I wouldn't have time to grieve, though, because a short time later, I had to be strong for my husband and children, my husband lost his hero, his father, after a terrible battle with cancer. We were shattered; a couple of nights before his passing, my husband and I moved our little family to where his dads place was. The original plan was to take care of him. To begin with, it was hard being there without him; as the months passed, things for the family got easier. I will finish school in the spring of 2020 and receive a career diploma in Wildlife and Forestry Conservation. With this I can assist my husband with diagnosing common tree diseases. I am also still the secretary for the business. I tried to go to school for accounting in the coming years, but it was like Greek to me so I'll stick to what I know. 2020 would bring another change into our lives besides the disastrous pandemic; with everything happening with the public school system, I decided to pull all four of our children out and homeschool them and Windy Hollow Academy was born. What a challenge that was, as the months went on , the children and I began to get comfortable in a routine. I started to enjoy homeschooling them; it was not as bad or difficult as I thought. After the first month or two, I decided to return to school for child psychology. I thought if I'm going to homeschool these guys, I need to get an idea of how their brains work. For the rest of the school year, I would give the children their assignments and I would go and work on my studies. The program I used to homeschool them had certified teachers with each subject which was great because I could give out assignments, but I am not teaching material. With that program, I was confident the children would learn everything they needed to. I would take Fridays off and use that day as a science experience day, it was a win-win. The children learned about science and received extra credit for participating. We would take a coup ofle short vacations with the children, it was always nice spending quality time with them. The year would end, and 2021 would begin, 2021 would bring more heartache and pain, a few sweet accomplishments, and end with a broken family. That winter, I would lose an uncle whom I admire greatly. I had already lost one to a tragedy, but this was different. I watched him go through pain and agony. I was with him when we found out about my grandmother's passing. It wasn't too long after that my husband would experience two more losses. I wouldn't say I liked how 2021 was shaping up, all this loss in such a short time, within the first five months. I would obtain my certificate in Child Psychology from Penn Foster Career School that May. The second half of the year would have some happy moments with the children and a much needed day with my other grandmother. I surprised them and showed up just to spend time with them that day. The last time was when I lost my grandmother the previous year, and once more, when I got my graduation attire and first career diploma. I would tell my grandparents about my plans and my little family. I felt something wasn't right with my grandmother from the start. Of course, I didn't bring it up, but I knew and would soon have my suspicions confirmed. The rest of the summer would end, and homeschooling '22 would start back up. For the first two months of school, things went well; everyone was doing great. In

October though, we would have a problematic experience with my daughter. A couple years ago, in 2017, she got sick with a cold, which quickly turned into mycoplasma pneumonia. With that came a high fever that caused her to have her first seizure episode. We manage medications, but there are times when she goes into a bad one. That day in October 2021. I rushed her to the hospital, and she was admitted for a week. This was the second time we had been admitted for these episodes. They are scary, I have seizures, but mine are way different than hers. The first time we stayed, I told myself no more screwing up; this child needed me there all the time I needed to be her rock, and that's what I have become. This second time with her, I barely left her side. When the episodes happen, she can be numb for days, unable to walk, talk, hold anything. I recently learned what she experiences is called Todd's Paralysis. It breaks my heart when they happen. I have accepted, though, it's just a part of our world, our story and I am prepared and vigilant. Some would say I am overprotective, but I don't want to lose my baby girl. We came home from the hospital on Halloween. I feel bad because that year, I didn't take her trick or treating. Normally it wouldn't have mattered, but by then, I learned of my grandmother's prognosis, which wasn't good. I wish I had just carried her out to the truck and taken her up there anyway, so we could have seen her one last time as we knew her. Halloween would be her last best night. The holidays would arrive soon after, and we would lose my grandmother a few weeks before Christmas. Once again, we were heartbroken. By the end of year, my little family would become a broken one; my husband's oldest daughter Gracie celebrated her sixteenth birthday in a big way, she ran away from home. We were all shattered, but she was found safe and sound and would get sent to a group home; in time, we would learn the truth behind her behavior. She wanted her mom. I understood that because well, for so long, I was separated from Myranda, my own doing unfortunately, but I understood. There will be a period of noncommunication between her and us. We both loved her and only wanted the best for her. That Christmas was a sad one for all of us. I faked it through Christmas day, took down everything, and threw out the tree. We had enough holiday spirit for one year. 2022 would prove to be a whole other year for us. The business we were running was prospering, it felt good to be getting ahead in life. I would go on a family vacation with my best friend and all her children to Tennessee that summer. They had passes for dollywood, so we went for a few days. It felt good having my best friend back in my life. We had about a 6-8 year time span that we didn't talk about. Also that summer, we would have a couple of house guests. My bonus daughter Brooke, and her daughter Avea. Brooke and I started to get close, we had already been close for years but this time, things were different. She became my biggest cheerleader, my biggest helper, and if the truth is being told, my best friend. She helped me plan my vow renewal to my husband. That's right, 2022 was a milestone year. Ten years since hubby and I said our "I dos". I wanted to renew our vows because we had been through so much that I figured it was time for a "start over," so to speak. She would be my rock during those months of planning, everytime something would go wrong, I would find her and vent. I took September off from the wedding long enough to celebrate another big accomplishment, ten years sober. Yes, I know the first five were sketchy, but i was told once, "Dust yourself off and keep going". The last five years, though, through the heartache, the pain, I stayed sober. I fight every day to stay sober, I'll never stop fighting. I would receive my ten year chip shortly after my 36th birthday; I held it in my hand, looked in the mirror and said "girl, you did it; you did what they said you couldn't, now go change the world, it's time to tell your story" with that, I transformed myself into who i am today, i am the one who rose from the ashes, and I will never let anyone try to stop me. The next month, October 2022, would be one of my favorite months of the whole year. I would have my vow renewal ceremony, my children were all involved and I had the cutest, sweetest flower girl, bonus granddaughter, Avea. That wedding would make so many of my dreams come true, all our children, but one were a part of the ceremony, my father would give me away, and my family showed up to support us, and I would be making up for everything the past ten years and start fresh with my husband, i love him wholeheartedly, and this was my way of showing it. We recited our own vows; everything was perfect. I will forever remember that day with smiles.That night I would have the sweetest dance with my step son, he was 15 then, and i told him to pick out the song, and he did; it was a real tear-jerker. The next day, the hubby and I started out for our honeymoon. On the road we talked and this or that; I let him know that I was ready to begin another phase in my life, that I was going back to school, and that sometimes, there are some people who can't handle the truth. I feel horrible for who I was then, but I can say that the girl from my past no longer resides inside me, and the woman that replaced her is much more powerful, she channeled all that hurt, the anger, the pain in an unstoppable force. I will do it literally during my honeymoon. I was anxious to get started. We would have an amazing honeymoon with a dolphin tour, a dolphin show, some great food, one tight climb up a lighthouse, and one romantic beach dance. At this moment, I am at peace. Christmas 2022 would bring our little family a miracle. For the first time in 6 long years, my stepsons would see their mother, she, too, had to go through a journey to recovery and her own series of unfortunate events. reuniting with her, our family has turned our family from broken, to whole again. I look forward to being able to celebrate the lives of our children together. 2023 would be a year of healing and being released from the chains of my past. For ten years, I worked on the 12 steps, there were a few that I had to grow mentally before I could take on, like making amends with those I wronged over the years. I also knew that I had to work to obtain that diploma I call "my baby," the one career diploma that means everything to me, my substance abuse counseling career diploma. During the honeymoon, I started the program. I was given a year to complete it, but for the next few months, earning that diploma would become my new addiction. I worked harder on it than anything else I had done to date. There were days that I would study for 12 hours at a time; thank goodness Brooke was there and took over as a homeschool assistant. With her help, I could complete the program in just over four months and receive my career diploma as a Social Services Assistant in Substance Abuse. I received my diploma in May 2023. With a straight A report card, a 4.0 GPA and graduated with Honors. I can't put into words the feeling of accomplishment that I feel. That's why I say never give up on your dreams. I didn't, and I won't. My children are forcing me to take this year (2023) off from continuing my education, so the rest of this year will be spent mending relationships. There are a few significant ones that need repaired for my soul to heal, and I am working on myself. I started the process of making amends with people via letters and personal videos and found out all too quickly not be a victim again, not at the hands of domestic violence, not from being sexually abused; I will no longer allow someone's negative energy to dwell inside my thoughts distorting them so that I am weak and vulnerable. This is my life and I own the rights to it. The videos brought healing to me and hurt, I learned there are some relationships I will never mend, and the damage has been done. I learned that i burnt several bridges over the years, and i had learned that when given a second chance, don't screw it up when my best friend Amber walked away from me after watching me get high while pregnant,it started the process of opening my eyes, but it would be several years before i heard from her again, in 2012 she decided after confirming my sobriety to come back into my life, it started little by little, and she is to this day my go to dairy. The love I have for her and her family only grows more and more with time. She keeps me grounded, and I am her go to for support. When she returned to my life, I knew I had to straighten my act up. The hardest pill I had to swallow happened when I learned the bitch of not being able to change the past or foresee the future. There was one guy Kent that I didn't get to apologize to for the past, which broke my heart. I posted the video on his memorial page. I want his family to know that if I contributed to his circumstances, he battled cancer for several years, and I truly was sorry. I had a hand in him going back to prison after all. With that, I sent the videos to a handful of people, many of whom are described in this book. I need them to know that I am not who I used to be and I am truly very sorry for all the pain I caused. I suffer from survivor guilt, there are many nights that I should not have made it, but I did. I also feel bad that I didn't care who I got high with, I was in my early 20s and getting high with teenagers, a few of them have either died or lived in full addiction. It breaks my heart that I was that bad off back then and contributed to others habits. It is through the amends process that I will receive the best gift that my life had to offer; as I am writing this book, I send Buck the chapter about "never, over" and unfortunately he doesn't remember too much of our time together due to his addictions, he too has been on a journey into recovery for the last 4 years. We talk on occasion now; things are way different than ever before. We value our friendship, but I needed to heal from our past so I asked him to release me from our pact "never over ". He told me that he forgave me years ago for everything, neither of us is who we were back then, and that only these last four years are what he would like to think of our friendship as. I explained my side more and for the first time since our meeting with him in 2009, I was released from that contract that bound my heart and soul for so long. With this newfound freedom, I am finally able to find myself. I can finally give my husband all of me, he has only gotten a portion of me since 2012, but I would commit to dedicating all my love energy into my marriage and creative energy to writing again. I have more education plans after this year's long break is over. I am going to go back to school to start working on my paralegal studies. When I finish, I will have spent five more years in college and obtained 4 more diplomas/certificates. My objective is to be a part of those that advocate for people who suffer from addiction and mental illness. I am proof that recovery and change are possible; I want to help people out of the trenches to become a better version of themselves. My work is just beginning. I will continue on making notes of the significant events throughout this journey, and who knows, maybe in a few years, there will be a follow-up book highlighting my accomplishments and challenges. No matter what, though, I am far from being done with my goals. As I close this chapter I leave you with the words of Cher ``you haven't seen the last of me''.

A FEW WORDS OF ENCOURAGEMENT

I want to leave the reader of this book with a few things that I have learned along the way. My hope is that one day, my story will change someone's outlook on life. It is important for you to know that you are here for a purpose. That you do mean something to somebody and that your life has value. There are times of struggle. Yes, life is not a picnic, but use those struggles to become a better version of yourself. We were not meant to live in the gutter or trenches, we were meant to survive and thrive. I believe those that have lived the roughest lives, seem to have the best stories. Truly an inspiration, the power of a comeback. Someone told me that with each new day, it is a new sheet of paper, a fresh start., a clean slate.I challenge you to look within yourself and ask yourself this, are you content with who you are now, or do you need a change? It's never too late to turn the page and begin a brand new chapter.

LETTER FROM THE AUTHOR

Dear Reader,

I hope that you enjoyed reading Product Of A Misspent Youth. If you take anything from this book I hope it is this, know that there is always a way out, you just have to find that glimmer of a light. Every day is a new beginning so treat it as such, don't spend too much time in the past, forgive yourself and move on. Never give up, that's the most important, Never give up, no matter how bad things get, don't give up. We are born fighters, just gotta tap into it every now and then. Set goals, then achieve them, baby steps that's all it takes, one step at a time. It's true what they say "One Day At A Time ", it really is day by day,second by second,moment to moment. Life is short, I have seen way too many die young, so live each day as if it was going to be your last. Let go of what you can't control and manage the rest. It's ok to struggle, just keep going. There is always a brighter future waiting once you are ready to step into the light. I hope that if anything reading this book might have made you think about something in your life that needs changing and I hope that you take those first steps to whatever it is that will make you feel whole again. Recovery is possible, healing is possible, having a good future is possible, you just have to want it bad enough. It is my 100 % belief that everyone is capable of recovery. Always remember, this isn't a race, the only prize you will win is your own sobriety and peace of mind.

Melissa